HAUNTED TALES FROM
THE REGION

HAUNTED TALES FROM
THE REGION

GHOSTS OF INDIANA'S SOUTH SHORE

DOROTHY SALVO DAVIS

Published by Haunted America

A Division of The History Press

Charleston, SC 29403

www.historypress.net

Copyright © 2010 by Dorothy Salvo Davis

All rights reserved

First published 2010

Manufactured in the United States

ISBN 978.1.59629.917.7

Davis, Dorothy Salvo.

Haunted tales from the region : ghosts of Indiana's south shore / Dorothy Salvo Davis.

p. cm.

ISBN 978-1-59629-917-7

1. Ghosts--Indiana. 2. Haunted places--Indiana. I. Title. II. Title: Ghosts of Indiana's
south shore.

BF1472.U6D3785 2010

133.109772'9--dc22

2010032461

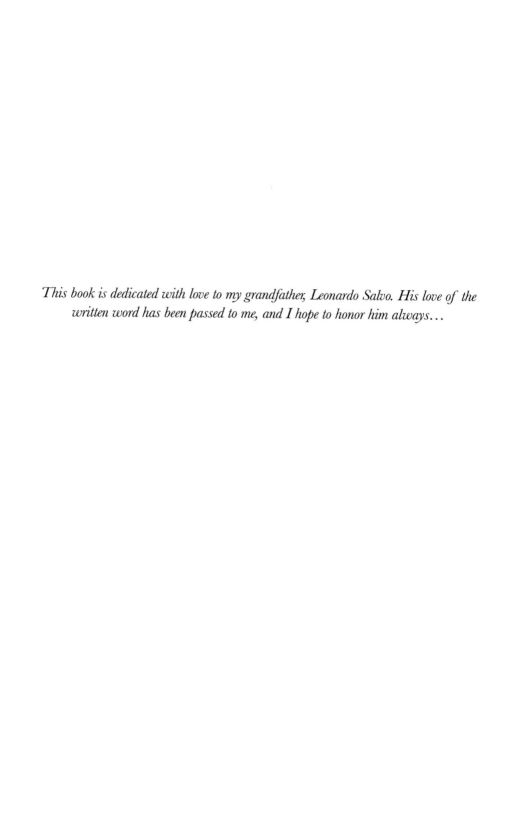

This book is dedicated with love to my grandfather, Leonardo Salvo. His love of the written word has been passed to me, and I hope to honor him always…

CONTENTS

CONTENTS

ACKNOWLEDGEMENTS

The cities in this book have done a sensational job in maintaining their history through their historical societies and libraries. Thank you to the staff at the Notre Dame University archives for preserving information on the surrounding area's past. The Indiana Dunes is a national asset, and it is being fabulously maintained. The education that the park passes on to our youth is invaluable.

A special thank-you is due to those individuals who were willing to share their stories. Paranormal encounters often leave the victim feeling ashamed and unable to share what occurred for fear of criticism. To those who allowed me to interview them, I admire your courage.

In closing, I must mention my very supportive family. Chris, thank you for listening to endless accounts of ghostly encounters. Josie and Conner, you keep me laughing; I need that when spending so much time researching the paranormal. My kids, I owe you for my endless joy. To my role model, Paolo Salvo, what can I say but thank you, Dad. Thank you Mom for reading to me so much as a child! You started me on a lifelong love for reading and writing. If not for you, my career as an author may not have happened.

INTRODUCTION

Northwest Indiana is also known as the South Shore. Many of the cities in The Region are considered suburbs of the Chicago area. The cities in the northwest area of Indiana have bred many great individuals who have reached celebrity status, forever becoming immortal in the area's past. Gary boasts the honor of raising the King of Pop, Michael Jackson. Crown Point holds the blemish of having had John Dillinger escape from jail in 1934. Both positive and negative events forever left a mark on the area. After all, the state of Indiana did not get to where it is today without a lot of hard work, sacrifice, love and loss, as well as scandal.

Events unfolded on the rich land of the Hoosier State that forever changed the outcome of our country's future. Northwest Indiana claimed several forts in the state's early years. The risk involved for the brave settlers who ran these communities was high. Often they were attacked by native tribes. In the end, sons, fathers and brothers of both white man and red were forever taken from their love ones.

The unbelievable struggle these people must have experienced has been imprinted on the land. The area has raised strong and determined men and woman who strive to stand against injustices. Indiana played a large role in the Underground Railroad. Other tragedies—such as the Revolutionary War battle at Fort Le Petit that took place on December 5, 1780, in the Indiana Dunes or the Spanish influenza epidemic of 1918—were devastating situations that one would prefer to leave in the past.

Unfortunately, the unpleasantness of the past won't disappear silently into Indiana history. The supposedly peaceful Hoosier State is alive with ghost stories both horrific and romantically eerie.

In Crown Point, Indiana, stands a beautiful Victorian-style home that was once the area jail and sheriff's home. The most famous prisoner of the past is John Dillinger, who knocked out the sheriff holding him prisoner in 1934. After beating the sheriff unconscious, Dillinger is said to have left, grabbing machine guns and leaving the sheriff bleeding and locked in a cell on the floor. Today, those who pass by the old home claim to hear an unexpected gunshot go off midday. A man walking his dog past the home claims to have been knocked flat on his back by an unseen force. Could the emotion of Dillinger's escape have been so great that it replays itself repeatedly in a residual haunting? Explore this and other claims of paranormal experiences that seem to have some connection to the past of northwest Indiana.

PART I
MICHIGAN CITY

TRYON FARM GUEST HOUSE

Staying at the Tryon Farm Guest House is a certain cure for stress. This bed-and-breakfast is a refreshing example of the way a B&B should be run. A very well-executed conversion of a charming century-old brick farmhouse into a modern bed-and-breakfast without losing any of the past has been accomplished. Mary and Scott stayed at the inn for their twenty-first anniversary and fell in love all over again. The couple had been under a lot of stress during the months leading up to their anniversary. Their youngest of three children had just left home for college. They were alone together a lot now. They realized that without the kids at home, they had nothing in common anymore. Their lives had revolved around their children. Mary and Scott had grown apart. Seeing the tension between their parents, their grown children pooled together and reserved their accommodations at the Tryon Farm Guest House.

Scott was not looking forward to the trip and fought with Mary on the long drive from Detroit to Michigan City. They fought about foolish things like the radio and speed limits. This was going to be a very long weekend. Both Mary and Scott were secretly thinking to themselves that a perfect anniversary present would have been separate vacations. Mary wondered to herself, "Where did the romance go?"

They pulled into the bed-and-breakfast on a sunny and warm Friday morning. The scenery that welcomed them was calming to their senses.

Michigan City Welcome Sign.

The 1896 Victorian farmhouse was beautiful and inviting. Mary felt a strong feeling of nostalgia. Scott was feeling like he'd been there before, although he knew that this was his first visit. When they entered the home, they were welcomed by the woman who ran the bed-and-breakfast. Her warm personality was contagious. She was very polite and made the couple feel right at home. Mary remembers the smell of fresh baked goods that just seemed to put the finishing touches on the moment. She felt like she was on the set of an old Hallmark movie.

Once they were settled in the immaculate and perfectly decorated Oak Room, they decided to take a walk. Neither one knows the exact moment when their feeling for each other warmed up, but they did. Scott took Mary's hand and led her outside to the grounds. Everything about the afternoon seemed perfect. They laughed and talked like they were teenagers again. Later, they enjoyed an amazing meal and retired to their room. As they snuggled in bed that night, plans for the future were made. Both fell asleep feeling at peace.

As Mary slept, she had a very detailed and vivid dream. She saw herself wearing an early 1900s-style farm dress. She was feeding chickens, which roamed free in front of her home. Strong arms wrapped around her waist, and she turned around, smiling. Her eyes met with Scott's and they kissed. Hearing a girl's laughter, she looked in the direction of the house. Coming out the door was their daughter. Mary doesn't know how she knew it, but she was certain that the girl was theirs. The house, Mary realized, was the Tyron Farm Guest House! Weird as it may seem, she knew that she was dreaming as she watched.

The sound of Scott's voice woke her from her heavenly slumber. He was sitting up in bed and trying to get a word out but couldn't form it. Looking in the direction he was staring, she saw a light mist evaporating into the night.

This woke her up fully and she reached for a light. Scott told her that he had just seen a woman in early 1900s-era clothing standing at the foot of the bed. She had to be about sixteen-years-old and resembled Mary. The apparition had just been staring at the sleeping couple. Scott said that he felt startled but not afraid, and his shock made it impossible for him to form words. Mary shared her dream with Scott. Somehow, they knew that this place would always be special to them. They were certain that they were meant to come to the Tyron Farm Guest House at this time in their lives.

The next morning, they had the best breakfast either of them had ever had. Saying goodbye to their host, they kept the story of their nightly visitor to themselves. Scott and Mary had three sons and no daughters. Could the young woman they had seen have been their daughter in a past life? Regardless, they were in love all over again. Scott and Mary believe that they have their children to thank. All of their children.

BLUE CHIP CASINO

The trip to the Blue Chip Casino in Michigan City, Indiana, had been planned for months. Dan and Linda had invited their closest friends, the Dekkers, to join them for a weekend of fun at the casino. Both couples were in their early to mid-forties and had been friends for more than a

Blue Chip Casino.

decade. They all worked forty-hours-per-week factory jobs in Lafayette, Indiana. As the kids were home with the grandparents, the weekend ahead was certain to be fun. They had planned enjoying the gambling, shows and, of course, fantastic buffets the casino offered. This was certain to be a wonderful weekend.

The Dekkers were very interested in the paranormal and had brought along a Ouija board hoping to get their friends to play. Linda never believed in the claims of ghost sightings. She was in her late twenties and married when she had her first possible paranormal experience. Their rental home had a strange noise coming from within a central wall. This went on for weeks until an investigation in the home's crawl spaces found that there was an old closed-up fireplace in the home. The spook turned out to be a bird that had gotten trapped inside. The poor thing had simply flown down the old chimney opening and had gotten itself stuck inside. After that, she believed that all paranormal encounters could be explained away.

Now, almost fifteen years later, Linda would change her mind. On the first night at the casino, she and her husband Dan went out with the Dekkers. After a fun night of music, food and drinking, Mr. Dekker decided to bring out a Ouija board to play with as they lounged in Dan and Linda's room. They were all very excited to use it, especially Linda, who had always wanted to try one.

They started their session with Mrs. Dekker and Dan touching the planchette. Linda was making jokes as the others looked at the board seriously. They started off by asking the normal questions: "Is anybody there?"…"Does anyone want to talk?" and more. They didn't receive any responses, and after running out of ideas, Mrs. Dekker asked Linda if there was anyone she wanted to talk to. Linda's mother had passed away three years prior, so she decided that she wanted to try and communicate with her. "Mom?" Finally, after a short time, the board responded with a "YES." They all got excited, and the normal blame game of "You're moving it!" started along, with a slightly drunk Mr. Dekker calling bulls--- as a spectator.

Not really believing it, Linda put her hands on the planchette and called out, "Hi, how are you? I've missed you so much." After a while, the board spelled out "STOP PLAYING WITH THIS RIGHT NOW." The air in the room seemed to change and feel heavy. The temperature dropped at least ten degrees. Despite many tries at attempting to get a response for more information, none came. The board didn't work after that. Linda continued to call out to her mom, but the planchette didn't budge. They gave up and continued their night; eventually, the Dekkers left later that evening. They left the game open on the floor where they had earlier been playing.

Dan and Linda were exhausted and decided to go to bed. Shortly after falling asleep, Linda awoke. She opened her eyes to find her mother sitting at her bedside, staring at her! Her mother was wearing a lovely purple floral dress that she had been buried in, and her hair was short, framing her golden bronzed-colored face. Linda was now more fully awake but was too afraid to talk. Her frozen silence didn't matter because the ghost decided to speak in Spanish, in a firm but not really threatening way, almost a warning: "Linda, I am at rest. I am happy. Believe it is dangerous to disturb the dead. I was not the only one with you today. Never play that game again. Never!" Then she vanished, leaving Linda shaken.

As Linda cried, she woke up Dan by shaking him without mercy until he sat up. She told him what happened, and he had to hold her for the rest of the night. Linda knew that he didn't believe her but sought the comfort of his arms surrounding her.

The next morning, she told Dan that her mother told her that she should never play a Ouija board ever again. Dan tried to assure her that she imagined the whole event. She was, after all, slightly intoxicated when she fell asleep. To Dan, it made perfect sense that she would imagine the event. To Linda, the sight of her mother sitting on her bed and glancing down at her was too vivid in her mind. She was confident that it really happened.

Later that afternoon, the two couples were enjoying some slots in the casino when Linda felt someone grab her left elbow and squeeze. Looking to her left, she was surprised to find an empty seat at the penny slot beside her. No one was nearby, as the other members of her small group had gravitated to other areas of the gambling floor.

This unnerved Linda after the night she just had. She made her way to the restroom, and right before entering, a woman in a baby-soft blue sundress with waist-length red hair exited. The beautiful woman stood out in the crowd, and it would have been impossible for her to not be noticed by anyone. When Linda entered the restroom, she stopped in her tracks. Standing directly in front of her was the woman in blue whom she had just passed on her way in. This beautiful woman grinned as she looked Linda in the eye for what seemed like a eternity. Then she seemed to dissolve into a mist and vanish. Oddly, being in the busy casino, she was standing alone in the restroom. The temperature around her seemed to get cold, and the water faucets turned on. Her only instinct then was to turn and leave.

Amazing to Linda, she did not faint, but she did leave the gambling floor, grabbing Dan on her way. She seemed unreasonable, and Dan had never seen her so unnerved before. Despite his wanting to stay, he did not argue when she demanded that they leave the casino and return home. Leaving her in the room to pack, he returned to the gambling floor to let their friends know of their early departure. As Linda packed their bags, the lights in the room started to flicker. Standing still, she felt a chill go up her spine, and a soft voice whispered in her ear, "You call?" Then the Ouija board that had been left on the floor levitated up and flew into the nearby wall. That was enough for Linda. Leaving everything, she grabbed the car keys and headed out of the hotel as fast as her feet would carry her. Dan found her sitting in the car looking pale and extremely shaken.

After returning home, no strange events occurred. Nothing seemed to follow Linda, but she still wonders who the woman was who seems to haunt the Blue Chip Casino. Was she an evil entity or simply a lost soul? Whatever haunts the casino, Linda has decided to take her mom's advice from the grave and not seek contact again.

The Creek Wood Inn

Randy was staying at the Creek Wood Inn with a few friends from work in the summer of 2007. They were enjoying the fishing of Lake Michigan and the nearby golf courses. This was a boys-only trip, and they certainly were living it up, enjoying the recreation all day and casual drinking and games at night. The scenery at the inn was very relaxing. Everything about the location was neat and tidy. Randy found himself the most relaxed that he'd been in years.

Randy was an accountant and handled corporate accounts. His work often left him tense and stressed. For the last few years, Randy had a very difficult time sleeping. He suffered from insomnia most nights. Every night, Randy would lay his five-foot-seven-inch body down and settle under the covers. His dark eyes would stare at the ceiling as he thought about the many things he'd have to do the next day. He tried every old wives' tale that he'd heard to help him sleep, but none worked. Despite the suggestion of sleeping pills, Randy continued to stubbornly look for natural cures for his insomnia. He never imagined that something paranormal would cure his sleeping dilemma.

When Randy was getting settled into his bed at the Creek Wood Inn on his second night's stay, it dawned on him that he'd slept through the previous night. He realized that he didn't get up and lie down or toss and turn as he normally did. The time was just after midnight, and the alarm was set for six o'clock in the morning. Randy was meeting his friends early to do some fishing. Pulling the covers up to his chin, he hoped for another night of restful sleep. As was his nightly ritual, he said his prayers out loud in the room. Closing his prayers for the night, Randy said, "Amen." That is when he heard it. The disembodied voice of a man repeated his Amen. Despite his mind telling him that he was alone, his head was suddenly feeling very heavy. The next thing he knew, it was morning.

Randy had slept through another night in a deep sleep. Sitting up in bed, he stretched his arms and looked around the room. At first, he just felt that something was different. He couldn't put his finger on it, but there was something that just didn't seem the same as the night before. Then he realized that the dirty clothes he had placed in a pile on the floor were folded on a chair. He stood up and walked right over to the neatly folded pile of his dirty clothes. How come his dirty laundry was folded? Picking up the top polo shirt, Randy realized that it had a very fresh scent to it. The smell reminded him of the soap his grandmother had used when he was a child. How did his clothing get washed and folded? He knew that he didn't do it and that there was no one else who would have been with him.

That was when he remembered the echoed sound of the Amen the night before. Not sure what to make of it, Randy dressed and left the room to join his friends. Well, fishing that morning with his friends, Randy told them of the strange voice and his laundry. They had a good laugh at Randy's story and spent the rest of the morning teasing him that he must have a ghostly roommate. The day went by very fast, as most vacation days do, and Randy was alone in his room again before he knew it. Still, he felt completely comfortable and not at all uneasy.

Randy said his prayers without anyone echoing him and fell fast asleep once again. He had slept so soundly that his alarm didn't even wake him in the morning. He woke to the sound of his friend Josh knocking on his door. Standing up, Randy noticed immediately that his shoes were placed neatly by a chair near the door. Catching his attention was the shine of his loafers. The shoes had been polished! Turning his head, Randy discovered that his shirt was laid neatly across the back, along with slacks, was too much for him. He pulled open his room's door to allow Josh inside.

Josh noticed right away that Randy seemed pale and thought that maybe he wasn't feeling well. Randy had sat back down on the bed and was rubbing his temples. He wasn't frightened by what was happening—just very puzzled and confused. He took a moment to refocus and told Josh that he would be just a minute. Stepping into the bathroom, he found his shaving supplies and toothbrush all organized and laid out for his use. He went to Josh right away and pulled him into the bathroom to look. Josh really seemed to not believe Randy and acted as if the whole matter was some kind of joke. Not enjoying the banter, Randy decided to pretend like he was playing a practical joke. He absolutely didn't want to be teased by the other guys about things that go bump in the night again. When they joined the others, Randy never mentioned his strange situation again.

That night, Randy went back to his room for his last night's sleep at the Creek Wood Inn. They were heading back to Chicago in the morning. He was afraid that he would feel uneasy in his room alone that night, but he was very comfortable. He went to bed and said his prayers, and as his mind wandered toward sleep, Randy said aloud, "Butler, I won't be needing your assistance tonight. Please take the evening off." He meant it as a lighthearted joke as he drifted off to another peaceful slumber.

The next morning, when he woke, everything was just as he left it. Packing his final items away in his suitcase, he laughed to himself. Randy wondered if his giving the "butler" the night off was such a good idea. He was awful at packing and could barely zip up his suitcase. He left the inn with no more paranormal encounters. He had one of the best vacations of his life. His stay at the Creek Wood Inn was the best sleep he ever got, even to this day. Randy credits his cure of insomnia to the spirit of the "butler" at the wonderful Creek Wood Inn.

Light House Premium Outlets

Over the years, there have been many claims of paranormal activity among the Light House Premium Outlet stores in Michigan City, Indiana. There have been reports of items being moved to full-blown apparitions appearing. The image of a small boy has been seen looking

A Light House Outlet store.

in the windows, and a lady in a long trench coat has been seen walking into the stores without even opening the door!

One rainy afternoon, a strange orb seemed to hover in front of the Aéropostale store. Staff said that they could not discern what it was or where it had come from, but it hovered for more than an hour. The staff reported that the orb appeared to assume a roughly anthropomorphic form at one point as it hovered out of the store's window/wall.

Sue Plunket, a former manager at a store within the outlet mall, said shortly after the sighting that the mysterious appearance of the entity began to appear. The image was that of a woman with long brown hair swept up into a ponytail. She wore a long tan trench coat tied around the waist. This woman didn't appear solid and shocked many shoppers when she appeared to enter the store right through a wall. The misty figure understandably has vexed Sue to this very day, but she says that nothing of this nature has ever happened before the lady apparition appeared. "It was happening every weekend at the same times. This went on for a few months before it suddenly just stopped." Sue didn't believe in ghosts but admitted that she couldn't explain what was happening. "There may have been some very strange things going on, but work went on as normal."

Sue said that she had reported the happening to her superiors and that they had wasted no time in telling her to not allow the situation to get out of hand. She was told to keep the matter quiet. Sue claims that there were other mysterious goings-on around the store. "We had a few cameras in the store, and they had been randomly switching off, but the date and time had remained on the screen." She went on to indicate that the lights, though on a timer, had been turning on by themselves when no one was in the store and the doors were locked. An investigation into who could be interfering turned up no leads.

There is, however, a theory that perhaps the ghost could be that of a deceased workman who was killed while renovations were going on throughout the area, which is alleged to be haunted, or it could be the mysterious spirits haunting the flat themselves. The lenses of the cameras had all been inspected and cleaned, yet footage has shown orbs and strange mists appearing. Many believe that the source, whatever it may be, isn't directly linked to any particular store as it has been seen in different ones.

Sue no longer works at the Light House outlet store she once managed but says that hopefully someone will sort out this disturbance once and for all, though local employees aren't complaining. Since the sightings, customers still move in and out of the place at will, unaware of the paranormal entity, and some who have gotten wind of the strange events are even curious about the mysterious figure being spotted in the area. Sue herself is curious about the identity of the lady in the trench coat and has heard from friends still employed in the area that she was not the only apparition to make an appearance. There have been reports of a little boy in jeans and a polo seen looking in the store. He presses his face up to the glass and just stares in. When someone goes outside to see if he is lost and looking for someone, he vanishes, leaving his imprint on the glass.

Regardless of whether you believe in ghosts, the Light House outlet stores are the perfect place to ghost hunt, as you can shop for all of the terrific bargains that the stores offer while you look.

Michigan City Old Lighthouse Museum

"Charming" and "quaint" are the first words that come to mind when first visiting the Old Lighthouse Museum in Michigan City, Indiana. The view beyond the lighthouse is breathtaking, and it easy to see why the lighthouse was constructed at the location it has occupied since 1858. In fact, the first lighthouse was built on the property in 1837. This location is indeed a place rich in history, a place that has a lingering sense of nostalgia. The past has not been forgotten here.

Upon meeting with Mr. X (as we will refer to him for his preferred privacy), I was immediately taken in by his stern gray eyes. Despite being in his early seventies, this man's eyes hadn't lost their fire or zest for life. Mr. X was at least six feet tall and had a large build. He could easily have been mistaken for Santa Clause with his full white beard and belly bulge. Still, his stance was straight and strong. He was in remarkably good condition for a man his age. When he boasted of being able to beat men half his age in arm wrestling, it was easily believed. Meeting with him over a cup of coffee for this interview, I confess to being slightly embarrassed when he barked his order at a timid waitress. This was a man who had no time for games and was very direct.

Not wasting any time, before we even got our coffee, Mr. X began his recollection of his time at the Old Lighthouse Museum. He was a carpenter by trade. During the late 1960s, he volunteered his services to work on the reconstruction of the old lighthouse, turning it into the museum it has become today. Growing up in the Michigan City area and having served eight years in the U.S. Navy, Mr. X hated to see the old lighthouse fall into disrepair. He was happy to be onboard in bringing the old structure back to life. He and several friends worked tirelessly during the summers on the lighthouse, taking care to respect its past.

Mr. X stated right off that prior to this experience he never believed in ghosts. In fact, he thought that anyone claiming to have seen or felt something paranormal was loopy and not right in the head. He used to feel that everything could be explained. He thought that wimps too afraid to seek the explanation settled on assuming that their paranormal experience had to be a ghost. Looking down for a moment, he became suddenly quiet. Then he looked up, meeting this author in the eye. Very seriously, Mr. X said, "I always admit when I am wrong. I was wrong to ever think that there is no such thing as ghost!"

His personal experience started the very first night that he and another fellow were alone at the lighthouse. The time was nearing dusk, and they were cleaning up from a day of labor. Knowing that they were completely alone, the two men froze in place when they heard footsteps above them. Both men looked at each other and then instinctively headed in the direction of the sound. The footsteps seemed to be coming from the stairs leading up to the lighthouse lantern. As the two men made their fast approach to the top, they heard a noise coming from the top. The sound was like someone wiping glass. When the men reached the top, they found no one. Mr. X remembers that the air had an icy chill, and the other fellow commented on the lilac smell that lingered in the area. Finding no one at the top of the lighthouse lantern didn't put them at ease. After all, they were responsible for locking up. They spent the next thirty minutes searching the place and grounds. When they came back inside to collect their things, they were shocked to hear the sounds of footsteps coming down the stairs from the lantern area. Upon investigating, they again found no one. Only the sweet scent of lilac perfume drifted past the men again, with a cool breeze to follow.

At this point, Mr. X wasn't ready to blame anything on a ghost. He went home that night and racked his brain trying to solve the mystery of the footsteps. No easy answer came to him. Over the next several weeks, the footsteps continued to occur—and always at dusk. The eerie smell of the lilac perfume always followed, too. This became a game to the men working at the lighthouse. By this time, most had heard the light footsteps go up to the light and thirty minutes later descend again. Each man would try to solve the mystery and secretly hoped to catch a pretty young thing wearing lilac perfume toying with them. Of course, no pretty young thing was ever to be found—alive that is.

Mr. X was going away one weekend for a family affair and wanted to get an early start each day the week before he was to leave. Talking some of the boys into arriving at 5:00 a.m. to start work at lighthouse before their other jobs was not hard. The project had become like a boys club to some of them. They had a great time getting together each afternoon and didn't mind starting their days with some hard work and laughs. The very first morning that the crew of five arrived, the mystery footsteps appeared with a surprise. The time was dawn, and the men suddenly heard the light footsteps going up the stairs to the lantern. They decided that they would spread out along the steps to catch whomever it was coming back down thirty minutes later. Finding only humor and good clean fun in the situation, none expected to really find anyone. They were wrong on this particular morning.

Almost exactly ten minutes later, the men heard the sound of glass being wiped and smelled a strange burning odor they had not smelled before. They stayed very still and waited. Twenty minutes later, the sound of light footsteps were heard coming down. What happened next remained embedded in their minds for the rest of their lives. The image of a small petite woman with brown, auburn hair appeared. She looked as real as any one of them, except that she was slightly transparent. Her face was gentle and pretty. She wore her hair pulled up in a bun with a few loose curls escaping the sides. Her dress was a light green with little flowers and was buttoned from her neck to her ankles. As she passed each man, she nodded a polite smile. The men had their backs pressed firmly to the wall and tried desperately to not have their knees buckle below them. The sweet scent of lilac perfume followed her with a cool breeze. When she reached the bottom, she vanished!

The tough former military and naval men were like small boys again. Rushing together, they talked in astonishment about what they had just seen. Each was secretly afraid but none would admit it. Despite the appearance of the apparition, they didn't feel threatened, just uneasy. They continued to work on the lighthouse, but none ever allowed himself to be alone. The footsteps continued at dusk and dawn, but never during his time working on the lighthouse did Mr. X see the lovely apparition again. Her perfume was often smelled by the men, and occasionally tools would go missing only to turn up later. A few times, the tools were found in the lantern room when they were never brought up there by the living.

When his reminiscing was complete and his story told, Mr. X sat back in his chair. His piercing gray eyes found mine, and in an unsaid challenge he dared me to doubt him. I didn't dare! He was very adamant about the truth and accuracy of what he said. He closed by saying that if one doesn't believe in ghosts, he dares them to spend dusk and dawn sitting on the steps going up to the lantern room at the Old Lighthouse Museum.

Interestingly, there was a woman named Mrs. Harriet Colfax who was a lighthouse keeper for many years at the lighthouse. She fits the description of the woman Mr. X saw. When I showed him a picture of her, he pointed to her friend who resided at the lighthouse as the woman he and his friends saw that early dawn morning—and who turned him into a believer of the paranormal. Her name was Ann Hartwell. It certainly isn't hard to believe that she would assist in her friend's chores to maintain the lighthouse. They only saw one apparition, but perhaps they were in the presence of both of these fine women. Upon hearing Mr. X's story, it would be easy to assume that he was dealing with a residual haunting—a haunting that is simply an event of the past replaying itself, kind of like a recording. However, that the entity nodded and smiled a hello to the boys gives the impression that the entity is an intelligent haunting and is still very much on duty.

Following is some history and past newspaper articles about these very fascinating women, who may still linger at the lighthouse they so loved. The articles both prior to and following their deaths show the great love and appreciation the community had for them.

Chicago Tribune, *October 2, 1904.*
A Fragile Woman of 80 Years Is Uncle Sam's Oldest and Most Reliable Lighthouse Keeper.

The oldest, staunchest, and most reliable lighthouse keeper in the United States is a woman. A little, fragile, pretty maid of more than 80 years has broken the records of all lighthouse keepers in this country in length of service, in age, and above all, in the fact that her light never failed, never went out between the hours of sunset and sunrise during the forty-three years that she has tended it.

Her cousin, Schuyler Colfax, suggested the lighthouse of the little port in which she lived as a field for activities. She assumed control of the lighthouse and the old harbor beacon in the spring of 1861. Since the first day of her stewardship the great gleam of the harbor light has never failed to blaze across the waters at sunset, and never while the old beacon at the entrance of the harbor stood has she failed to flash its yellow radiance across the water before dark. At eventide each day during the navigation season for forty-three years she has replaced the waning lamp with a fresh one; at dawn for forty-three years she has quenched the beacon, and crept silently to her lonesome bed, happy in the sense of duty done, sure that the voiceless message of her unfailing light had carried courage and brought safety to many a ship and small boat tossed on the rough waters of Lake Michigan.

There were times when she was ill. There were nights when the groaning, wind driven seas lashed over the long pier that led to the harbor beacon. But she never failed. Drenched with icy spray, almost blown from the slippery footing, groping her way from the lighthouse to the beacon, across the wind swept sand dunes, floundering, tired with the burden of her big lamp, chilled with the blasts of belated spring or early winter, she never failed to keep the beacon bright and constant, never permitted the terrors of the storm or the fears of her womanly heart to deter her for a moment. "Little Miss Colfax's light." That's what the navigators have called the harbor light at Michigan City for forty years and so it will be known, perhaps, for forty years to come. For it was the most certain of them all. The old town set its clocks by "Miss Colfax's light"; the people of Michigan City rose by it, and to this day the gleam of the sunset light in the old house by the margin of Lake Michigan is as true to the moment of sunset as the clock to the calendar. She was seen at sunset the other evening trimming the great lamp in the tower above her lakeside home. She clipped the wicks and tried the burner, looked at her watch, and struck a match. "It is time," she said, lighting the lamp and smiling a happy smile. In an instant, the tiny, glass covered cage was filled with a fierce glare.

She still loves her work. "I am able to do the work, you see," she said in her thin, sweetly quavering voice. "I have a helper to carry up the lamps, but always trim and light them myself. In forty-three years none but me has done it. I love the lamps, the old lighthouse, and the work. They are the habit, the home, everything dear I have known for so long. I could not bear to see anyone else light my lamp. I would rather die here than live elsewhere. The work is easier now than it was once. Since the old beacon light was swept away I have but this main light to tend. In the old days they used lard oil for the lamps, and in cold weather we had to heat it. It was great trouble in cold weather to make the old beacon burn. The lard oil would get hard before I could get the lamp lighted, but once lit it never went out, you may be sure. My lights never went out till I quenched them myself." The slow moving, bowed old woman is proud of her record. The harbor light is in a glass cupola on the apex of the old house in which she lives, so that she can attend to her work in all kinds of weather without going outdoors. It was different in the old days when the beacon stood at the end of the government pier, half a mile from her house, and accessible only by a narrow walk, with a single rail to hold by. It was a stormy night toward the end of 1886 that Miss Colfax made her last trip to the beacon light. With her pail of heated oil in one hand and her lantern in the other she sallied forth into one of the most tumultuous storms that ever raged along the coast of Lake Michigan. The sleet stung her face, the furious wind drove the spray of the seas and the sand of the dunes pelting against her, and the darkness of the tempest fell so suddenly that she could hardly find the wave washed end of the pier. But she gained it, grasped the handrail, and, with head bent, struggled forward to the beacon tower. The waves dashed over and smote against the piling and woodwork of the pier till the timbers groaned and the frail woman could scarcely keep her footing. She fought her way along, gained the stairway, and in the shelter of the tower top filled the great lamp and lighted it. Then she came down, drenched to the skin, chilled to the bone, and for the first time, scared almost to fainting. The tornado had increased in fury, the slender stairway quaked beneath her, the tower wavered, and the noise of the wind and water was like the rending of a thousand sails. She had hardly gained the mainland when there was a grinding crash. She looked back in terror to see the great beacon, like some big meteor, whirl in an arc through the livid night and fall hissing into the lake.

All night she watched the tower above her own house praying that no ships would venture in, or that the main light, which she kept burning more brightly than ever, might guide them past the wreck of the beacon pier. And in the morning when daylight came, and she had snuffed the harbor light, she went down to the pier to see the ruin which the storm had wrought. The beacon tower was gone, half of the long pier had been dismantled, and the shore was strewn with the wreckage of a structure that had withstood the storms of fifteen years. "I have seen many storms," said Miss Colfax the other day, "but never one like that. I was sorry to lose the old beacon, in spite of all the trouble and danger it brought me, for I was getting fond of it, and it was a great help to the sailors who didn't know the old harbor entrance." That was eighteen years ago, and since then Miss Colfax has had only the regular light to look after. She lives in the lighthouse, a strong, square, homelike house, built for the harbor service in 1858. Only the big lantern like cupola on the top of it distinguishes it from any other cozy country home, and the dense grove which has grown up around it threatens to obscure the harbor light which now scarcely peers above the tall cottonwoods and willows. The house is hard by the margin of the lake, surrounded by a pretty garden and but a few steps from the fine park of Michigan City. But the hand of progress has been laid on the old lighthouse. In a few weeks more the beloved beacon will be quenched never to be relighted. Already a dozen government workmen are busy about the building. New porches, broader doors, new windows, and a score of modern improvements are being added. The little woman inside looks wistfully at these changes, but it is the knowledge that her beloved light is to be abolished that brings tears to her dim eyes and makes her low voice tremble.

In the house of Miss Colfax, her confidante and companion of seventy years, lives Miss Ann Hartwell, a tiny, slim, blue eyed woman with curly gray hair, infinitely gentle, and like her aged comrade in many ways. Passing the four score milestone together, these two quaint, lovable spinsters have been bosom friends since the days of their childhood in Ogdensburg, N.Y. Miss Hartwell was a pioneer school teacher of northern Indiana, she taught three generations of its people, and when old age and failing health brought an end to her work she went to the lighthouse to pass away her final years with "Harriet." Here they lived for many years, clinging to the old fashioned habits and methods of half a century ago. Winter and summer on Sunday mornings these two slow going, weary but dainty ladies can be seen wending away to church, arm in arm, dressed like the fashion plates of the ante-bellum days, smiling upon middle aged men and women who were their pupils forty years or more ago, cheering one another with gossip of the romances of the far time when they were belles of the same town in which they are now ending their peaceful lives. There is something almost childlike in the tenderness with which the two cronies love one another. "We have never quarreled, Harriet and I," Miss Ann will say. "And we never will, Ann," Miss Colfax will answer, taking the other's small, thin hand in hers. "Never! That is, unless you again insist on tending my light. That's one thing you or anyone else shall never do while I am lighthouse keeper."

And then the queer, guileless pair will laugh right heartily, smiling in each other's faces as though it were a merry topic.

But how long will Harriet Colfax, little Miss Harriet, be keeper if the Michigan light? Already three new beacons have been built. The new harbor light is at the end of a long, long pier, with a steam engine and boilers; furnaces to be fired, coal to be shoveled, fog horns to blow, winding ladders to climb, and work for three men to do. One of the beacon guide lights is on a detached breakwater far out in the harbor. It can be reached only in boats, and when the north winds blow that coast is beaten by the roughest waters of Lake Michigan. These new lights are nearly ready. The old one, the famous "Little Miss Colfax Light," is doomed. The wonderful little woman who keeps it knows that the days of her long service are soon to end.

"I have not spoken of resigning," she said. "I can't bear to leave the dear place and the old light. I expected to die here with Ann and the place just as they have been for so long."

Then, her bright brown eyes twinkling: "If I remain it will be necessary to have help, of course, but I would have all the responsibility, just as I have always had. It might be all right that way. But no. No. It can never be the same after my old light is gone. I don't know how I shall sleep, knowing that it is out and that I cannot light it again."

And then, if you will listen, she will tell you long forgotten tales of shipwrecks on the Indiana coast. Of storms that almost blew her into the lake; of castaways and rescues; of bold sailors who brought her presents in the days of her youth, and of how some famous captain praised the brightness of her light and the fidelity with which it always "showed." But of the romance of her own calm life, if there was one, she will say nothing. The town gossips say that ever so many years ago, when little Harriet Colfax was the prettiest schoolma'am in Michigan City, there was a—But Miss Colfax doesn't like this kind of gossip *about herself, and if you ask her she will change the subject. "What a dreadful noise the carpenters are making," she will suggest. "I suppose it is necessary, though. The place was good enough and I'm not fond of changes." And the hammers sound sad, too, when you remember that the little old lighthouse keeper is past 80, and that the great old light that she has tended for forty-three years is "going out" forever.*

Chicago Tribune, *October 2, 1904*
HARRIET COLFAX AND ANN HARTWELL

Harriet Colfax served as the keeper of the Michigan City Lighthouse for 43 years, from her appointment in 1861 until her retirement at age 80 in 1904. Miss Colfax was a native of Ogdensburg, New York where she had been a teacher of voice and piano. She moved to Michigan City in the 1850s with her brother who had founded a local political newspaper. Miss Colfax worked as a typesetter on the paper as well as a music teacher. Her brother sold the newspaper and moved from the area but Miss Colfax remained in Michigan City with her companion, Miss Ann C. Hartwell, also a teacher and native of Ogdensburg, New York. At age 37 Miss Colfax took up the lighthouse keeper's position. Harriet Colfax and Ann Hartwell, who were known to their friends as "Ann and Tat," spent the rest of their lives together, primarily in the Michigan City Lighthouse. In the late 1800s, after twenty-five years of teaching, Ann Hartwell ran a newsstand and bookstore in downtown Michigan City. Her bookstore had Michigan City's first circulating library. In 1894, Miss Hartwell was a founding director of the Michigan City Branch of the Needlework Guild of America, an organization providing clothing to those in need. Miss Colfax and Miss Hartwell were supporters of the Library Association and construction of the Michigan City Library which opened to the public on October 9, 1897.

Harriet Colfax died on April 16, 1905, shortly after the death of Ann Hartwell on January 22, 1905.

Mishawaka, Indiana newspaper, Friday, January 27, 1905
Ann Hartwell Obituary

Death Severs an Unique Companionship. In the death of Miss Ann C. Hartwell, which occurred at Michigan City on Sunday morning last, January 22d, in the 77th year of her age, the earthly career of a woman of more than ordinary gifts of mind and character, and a charming personality which had won a very wide circle of friends during a long and active life, came to a close. At the same time was ended so far as earthly associations are concerned, a life long companionship between two most worthy and estimable maiden ladies which has had few if any equals outside of the married state. Miss Hartwell was born in Beverly, Canada, August 2, 1828, a daughter of Col. And Mrs. J.K. Hartwell. Later the family moved to Ogdensburg, N.Y., where in childhood the deceased formed a strong youthful attachment for Miss Harriet E. Colfax. In 1854, Miss Hartwell went to Michigan City to reside in the family of her brother-in-law, Dr. M.G. Sherman. The previous year Miss Colfax had also moved to Michigan City, where her brother, Richard Colfax, had established a newspaper. Here the mutual affection of the two young ladies was resumed, resulting later in the twain forming a life partnership which continued for over a half century. Miss Hartwell for over 25 years was an efficient and deservedly popular teacher in the public schools of the city, while Miss Colfax taught music, until 1861, when, by the influence of her cousin, former Vice-President Schuyler Colfax, she was appointed keeper of the Michigan City lighthouse, which important position she filled for 43 years so well and faithfully as to have won a record which has been highly extolled in official circles, in the press and by the appreciative mariners.

All these years the two estimable maiden ladies continued their beautiful companionship. Last September, owing to the failing health of both, and changes in the local lighting service, Miss Colfax resigned her position. Both had been so ill the past few weeks that it was a question which might pass away first. That their reunion in that better land beyond the grave, cannot be long delayed is all too evident to the relatives and friends.

The high estimation in which Miss Hartwell was held in the community in which she had so long resided, was evidenced by the fitting eulogies pronounced by the local press, and the touching tribute paid her memory by Bishop John Hazen White in his sermon at the funeral on Tuesday afternoon.

The deceased was quite well known in Mishawaka, where she had frequently visited at the home of her niece, Mrs. E.A. Jernegan. The latter and her sister, Mrs. R.T. Van Pelt, were both brought up by Miss Hartwell after the death of their mother.

Michigan City Dispatch, *obituary, 1905, Miss Ann Hartwell*
One of Michigan City's Oldest and Well Known Residents

Called to Her Final Reward After a Lingering Illness—Hers Was an Active Life Identified With the History of the City. In the death of Miss Ann C. Hartwell another of Michigan City's old residents has been removed from our midst. Miss Hartwell died at her late home, 624 Washington street at 4 o'clock Sunday morning, January 22, 1905, being in the 77th year of her age. Death was caused from a general breaking down of the mental and physical systems, complete exhaustion snapping the slender cord by which life suspended for months past.

Deceased was a native of Canada, where she was born August 28, 1828, the daughter of Colonel and Mrs. Joseph Hartwell. During Miss Hartwell's childhood, in the late 30s, the family moved to the states, locating in Massachusetts, but later removed to Ogdensburg, New York, where the subject of the obituary grew to womanhood. In 1854 she came to Michigan City to make her home with the family of her sister, Dr. and Mrs. M.G. Sherman, one of the prominent families in the early days of our city. Miss Hartwell ever afterward made Michigan City her home where her brilliant mind and genial disposition endeared her in love and respect to all who knew her and especially so to the old families of the city who know her in her youth, brilliancy and active life.

In 1858, Miss Hartwell took up the occupation of school teaching and for more than a quarter of a century was identified with our schools as one of its best instructors. In her long association with the schools she taught the children and some of grandchildren of her early pupils. Her school work like all the work of her life, was of a high character, as it must necessarily have been to have maintained her standing with the schools for so many years.

Deceased was a devoted member of the Episcopal church with which she labored faithfully and incessantly from childhood. She was a woman of superior intelligence and activity, and was constantly identified in the church and social events of the city for the leadership in which she was ever in demand. Honorable, consistent and actuated always by the highest motives she won and held the admiration of her friends. Hers was a useful, well-spent life and all who came in touch with her could not but feel the influences of her excellent character, her bright, genial disposition. The world is better for her having lived.

In her early life, in Ogdensburg, she formed warm attachments for a girl friend, Miss Harriet E. Colfax, which attachments grew to a sisterly love. Miss Colfax came to Michigan City in 1853 and when Miss Hartwell came in 1854, the friendship which began in Ogdensburg was continued and the two women became inseparable life companions. In 1861, when Miss Colfax was appointed keeper of the lighthouse at this port the two went to the lighthouse to live, and for nearly 50 years they have lived together as would two devoted sisters. In the summer of 1904, when changes in the light service at this harbor made it necessary to abandon the main light Miss Colfax, at her own bidding, resigned the keepership of the lights, and the two women, who by prudent management saved from their earnings a comfortable competency for the remainder of their lives, removed to the city, where they have since made their home. Miss Colfax, like her life companion, has been feeble in health for the past year or more, and at times it has been uncertain as to which would be the first to be called. Even at the hour of death of Miss Hartwell the death angel was beckoning to her companion and friends at her bedside watched with anxiety lest the slender thread be snapped and she too would answer the call. Her condition is serious and while it has been her heart's desire that she be spared to give the final care to her weaker sister, this prayer having been granted, friends fear that she too will answer the final summons. She fully realizes her condition and her desire now is that she and her companion of more than 50 years may be laid away together.

The funeral of Miss Hartwell will be held Tuesday afternoon at 2 0'clock at Trinity cathedral, Bishop White officiating. Friends of Miss Hartwell may view the remains in the oratory at Bishop White's residence, Tuesday forenoon from 9 until 12 o'clock.

Relatives and friends who are in the city to attend the funeral of Miss Ann Hartwell are: Mr. and Mrs. H.G. Sleight and daughter, Miss Harriet of Terre Haute; Mrs. William Sooy-Smith, Riverside, Ill.; Mr. and Mrs. E.A. Jernegan and son Ralph, Mishawaka; Mrs. Clarence Boyle, Chicago; Mrs. George Hartwell, Laporte and Mr. W.W. Colfax, Wyandotte, Mich.

Michigan City Dispatch, *1905*
Mortuary Record

Miss A.C. Hartwell's funeral of the late Miss Ann C. Hartwell was held this afternoon from Trinity cathedral, Bishop White officiating. Many old friends and acquaintances were present to pay their loving respects to the memory of the deceased. The floral offerings were fitting and marked the esteem in which Miss Hartwell was held by her friends. The remains were placed in the Greenwood cemetery vault. Burial will take place later. The remarks of Bishop White in memory of the deceased were beautiful and impressive. He spoke feelingly and with a full sense that the life of the departed warranted the beautiful words he spoke.

The pall bearers were Frank H. Doran, Jared H. Orr, G.G. Oliver, Walter Vail, W.F. Woodson and C.J Rob.

The funeral of the late Miss Ann C. Hartwell was held this afternoon at 2 o'clock from Trinity cathedral. The services were conducted by Bishop John Hazen White, who made a short address on the life and character of the deceased, and despite the severe storm there was a large attendance of friends of the deceased. There were many beautiful floral offerings. The remains were placed in the receiving vault at Greenwood cemetery and will be interred later. The pallbearers were W.F. Woodson, Walter Vail, George G. Oliver, C.J. Robb, F.H. Doran and J.H. Orr.

New York Herald, *obituary, 1905*

Miss Colfax has died at 81. Miss Harriette E. Colfax, a cousin of former Vice-President Schuyler Colfax and forty-three years keeper of the Michigan City Lighthouse on Lake Michigan is dead, aged eighty-

one years. Until her retirement last fall, Miss Colfax was the oldest lighthouse keeper in the United States' service. She had a remarkable record, the big reflector in her lighthouse never having failed to burn.

Michigan City Dispatch, *obituary*

Miss Harriet E. Colfax, After Lingering Struggle Yields Up Her Spirit to the God…

Funeral Wednesday Afternoon although for more than a year in failing health and for many months past lingering upon the brink of the unknown, into which she passed with unshaken faith in her Redeemer, the announcement of the death of Miss Harriet E. Colfax came with no less sorrow to her many friends, when, on Sunday evening her spirit peacefully took its flight to that home beyond. Death came from a general breaking down of the physical system and the gradual giving way of life's energies. Miss Colfax had been feeble for more than a year and her condition for three months past had been precarious.

The deceased was perhaps one of the best known ladies in the state of Indiana or around the great lakes, and had received through her identification with the government lighthouse service perhaps more newspaper prominence throughout the country than any other one employee of the government. For more than 43 years she was the faithful keeper of the guiding light at the port of Michigan City which in its unfaltering, never failing sentry, in calm and in storm, safely guided thousands of wayfaring mariners into port. It was only from failing health that less than a year ago she gave up her long and faithful lighthouse watch, and after nearly a half century of unerring and at times courageous and heroic duties, she relinquished her work and retired to a quiet, private home with the friend and companion of her lifetime, the late Miss Ann C. Hartwell. Only a few weeks ago, her companion passed to that home beyond, and since that time she has almost hourly been awaiting the death angel's call to join her devoted and beloved friend in the Father's mansion.

Soon after Miss Colfax had relinquished her duties at the lighthouse she was the recipient of the following letters, which in view of the fact that the government rarely ever turns aside from its red tape routine of business to write such letters, may be taken as the highest testimonial or compliment that could have been given her in recognition of her services. The letters read:

Letter of Thanks from Office of Chicago, Ill. To Miss Harriet E. Colfax…

Dear Madam:—I take great pleasure in forwarding herewith a letter from the lighthouse board dated Feb. 20, 1905, expressing its sympathy in your illness and its appreciation of your long and faithful service as keeper of Michigan City, Indiana light station.

While I was inspector but a short time of your period as keeper, I personally found all that the board, Admiral Watson and Mr. L. Morril states, to be true, and from my entrance on duty here all spoke of you in the highest terms.

Mr. Picking and myself join in wishing you health and happiness in your new location.

Respectfully yours,

F.E. Beatty, Commander, U.S.N.

Inspector, Ninth Lighthouse District Lighthouse Board, Washington, D.C., Feb. 20, 1905.

Miss Harriet E. Colfax, Late Keeper, Michigan City, Ind. Light Station.

Madam:—The board, learning of your illness, desires to send you an expression of its sympathy and its appreciation of your long and faithful service as keeper of Michigan City, Ind. Light Station. It appears from the board's records that in October, 1882, the inspector of the ninth lighthouse district, then commander, now Rear Admiral J.C. Watson, U.S.N., in asking authority for employing a temporary assistant keeper to aid you, stated in 1861, you had performed your duties in a most satisfactory manner.

It also appears that in March 1884, Mr. L. Morrill, surveyor, wrote from Michigan City, Ind., to a representative, asking him to bring to the attention of the board the necessity for an assistant to the station, describing the difficulties and dangers incident to tending the light at times, and referring to the fact that the position of assistant keeper had been abolished for lack of funds, and in his letter stated that "there is no person living more heroic and faithful in the discharge of a duty than Miss Colfax, as her 23 years of most devoted service as a lighthouse keeper is ample proof. She is absolutely wedded to the responsibilities of the position she has so honorably filled for nearly a quarter of a century, and in no one particular has she ever been charged with a neglect of duty nor is she ever likely to be, though she be left without help, as long as it is possible for any one person to discharge the duties devolving upon her."

This is a record of which you may well be proud which enables the board to thus commend you for the manner in which you performed the duties of the position you filled for so many years.
Respectfully,
Sherbee, Naval Secretary.

Harriet E. Colfax was the daughter of Richard W. and Phele…Seely Colfax, and was born in Ogdensburg, N.Y., December 3, 1824. She grew to womanhood and was educated in her native town. Her education included a fine training in music and she later became a music teacher of note, both in Ogdensburg and in her later home of Michigan City. She came to Michigan City in 1853 with her brother, R.W. Colfax, who was for many years publisher of the Transcript, Michigan City's only paper in those early days.

Through the efforts of Schuyler Colfax, who was in congress and who later became vice president of the United States, Miss Colfax was, in 1861 appointed lightkeeper at the port of Michigan City, which position she retained through all administrations, until she tendered her voluntary resignation in October, 1904.

Deceased was a woman of most amiable disposition and all acquaintances were her friends. She was consistent and faithful in her religious faith, being a devoted member of the Episcopal denomination.

She leaves of her family relatives, only one brother, W.W. Colfax of Wyandotte, Mich., to mourn her death.

Funeral Wednesday afternoon at 3 o'clock from Trinity cathedral. Friends wishing to view the remains may do so in the bishop's house where the remains will lie between 10 and 1 o'clock Wednesday. Funeral service in Trinity cathedral, Bishop White officiating. Interment in Greenwood cemetery.

Barker Mansion and Civic Center

Linda Stevens was fourteen the first time she experienced those butterflies a young girl gets for a boy. She remembers it like it was yesterday and not a decade ago. The day was a perfect 85-degree July afternoon with the sweet scent of flowers in the air. She had been dragged to a wedding by her parents for a cousin she didn't know. The wedding reception was held at the Barker Mansion. The mansion was breathtakingly beautiful. Originally, the mansion was built in 1886, and it was later renovated in 1929. The scenery was perfect for a wedding reception.

Exploring the mansion was the only thing Linda was looking forward to. After an hour of hellos and best wishes, Linda excused herself from her parents and walked outside to the gardens. The landscape was exquisite, and she remembers that being her start of a lifelong love for gardening.

She was enjoying the warmth of the afternoon sun on her face and the vibrant colors of the flowers when she suddenly heard the clearing

Barker Mansion.

of a throat, the way someone does when they politely want to make their presence known. Looking in the direction of the sound, her heart did a flip-flop. Only a few feet away was the most handsome young man she'd ever seen. For some reason, the word "debonair" came to mind when she looked at him. He was maybe sixteen or seventeen and had on the whitest button-down dress shirt Linda had ever seen. His slacks fit him perfectly, and his dark hair was combed over to one side in a old-fashioned kind of way. When he smiled at her, he had a strongly defined bone structure, with a dimple on both sides of his face.

Linda suddenly felt shy and awkward in her own skin. She smiled at him and said hello while a rush of butterflies soared through her. God, he was gorgeous, she thought. He reached a hand out to her politely and mouthed the word "Hello," but no sound could be heard. When she went to take his hand, hers grasped only air before her flesh touched his.

The handsome and perfect-looking young man had completely disappeared! She turned in a full circle, but he was no where to be found. All of a sudden, she felt dizzy and lightheaded. That was the last thing she remembered before hearing her mother's voice. Opening her eyes, she realized that she was lying on the soft grass beside a beautiful bed of bright flowers.

Her mother was obviously annoyed with her, thinking that she'd taken a nap out of boredom. She couldn't have been more wrong. Linda tried endlessly to convince her parents of what she'd seen, but they didn't believe her.

As an adult, Linda has toured the mansion a few times with hopes of a glimpse of the handsome boy she'd seen that July afternoon years before. For her, that was her first experience of a crush. Too bad he was not of flesh and blood.

On another occasion, a couple was touring the museum during the Christmas holidays. The wife had left the tour and had wandered alone into the library. When she entered the stunning room, she encountered a lady in perhaps her late thirties sitting in a chair. She said hello, but the lady did not look up from the needlepoint she was doing. The wife thought it was odd that the woman was dressed in obviously Victorian-era clothing. Feeling intrusive, she turned and found her church tour group.

After the tour was over, she asked the tour guide if they had an earlier reenactment? When she was told no, she proceeded to ask about the woman doing needlepoint in the library. The guide looked puzzled and assured the group that there was no one fitting that description there. Strangely, when the tour was over, the guide left at the same time. Could that have been the ghost of Mrs. Barker, who had passed away so young of illness?

On another occasion, several months later, the guide who had given the church tour was in the home alone closing up one evening. She heard a noise at the bottom of the main staircase: the sound of a gentle humming. Walking in the direction, she was stopped in her tracks by the silhouetted apparitions of a couple dancing. They appeared to be dancing a ballroom dance, and although the attire could not be seen clearly, as they were shadowed, the lady definitely had on a floor-length gown. The guide was frozen where she stood. Partly she was mesmerized but mostly was scared nearly to death, she confessed. The couple danced for what seemed like an eternity before vanishing, but in reality, they only danced for a minute after being discovered.

Even after they were gone, the humming continued until it seemed to fade away into the distance. The guide, to this day, doesn't know how she ever regained control of her feet. They seemed to have a mind of their own as she ran as fast as she could from the mansion.

WASHINGTON PARK ZOO

The Washington Park Zoo is a wonderful American zoo with more than two hundred animals. The zoo was originally founded in 1928. Built on fifteen acres, the zoo was started on a hilly sand dune close to the lake. This location has been an ideal location over the years. The zoo maintains clean grounds and fun activities each year that entertain thousands.

Della Harris worked at the zoo more than thirty years ago but remembers it as the best time of her life. She loved seeing the excitement on the children's faces. The best for Della was the animals. She'd always had a passion for animals and enjoyed being around them. According to Della, the zoo took exceptional care of the animals that resided there.

During the years she worked at the zoo, she heard talk of the ghost chimp often. The stories had started before she began employment at the zoo. People would claim that a chimp had gotten out of its cage. They would claim to see it wandering around among visitors. However, whenever anyone searched for the chimp, nothing was found. Of course, workers would always be certain to check that all chimps were accounted for in their cages. They always were.

Della remembers one afternoon when two women approached her excitedly. Carrying their toddlers, the women claimed that a chimp was in the tigers' area! They were afraid for the poor animal and demanded that she follow them. Just as she expected, when she inspected the area there was no chimp in the tigers' area. The women became very insistent of what they had seen. Della told them that they had simply witnessed the zoo's resident ghost.

Maybe the chimp was treated so well at the zoo during its life that it never left. Perhaps the chimp simply liked to entertain the zoo's visitors so much that it refused to move on. Whatever the reason, during Della's time at the zoo, the ghostly chimp encounters were always exciting news.

LAPORTE COUNTY COURTHOUSE

The courthouse is a beacon of joy for some entering its doors, but to others it is a place of life-changing choices. Ultimately, we all need a place to carry

LaPorte County
Courthouse.

out the just punishment of wrongdoers. Joe has worked as a custodian at the courthouse for many years. He watched people come in nervous and leave looking relieved. Sometimes they left in tears and handcuffs.

The emotions felt within the walls of the LaPorte County Courthouse are many. People have their lives changed here. If a choice about the outcome of their future is made that is not for the better, it is not hard to imagine that they may haunt the building after death.

Joe claims that reports of water turning on by unseen hands and toilets flushing are not uncommon. Doors that were locked the night before are open in the morning. Women have felt their hair tugged, and men have felt suddenly cold. No particular apparition has ever been reported. Joe is just happy that none was ever spotted while he was employed at the courthouse.

PART II
LA PORTE

LaPorte County Historical Society Museum

What makes a place haunted? The reasons for a haunting are many. A residual haunting, in theory, is just a strong emotional imprint left behind to replay over and over again. In fact, some locations have had awful, tragic events take place in which all parties involved were not deceased. Still, the emotion of the moment was so strong that it imprinted itself in time despite the fact that some in the group involved were still living. Perhaps a soul loved a location so much during life that it chose to stick around after death. Not just a place but also a person or object has been said to be haunted throughout history. Is it really so hard to believe that a person may have worked so hard on a home or shared laughter over a special tea set with loved ones that they choose to revisit the place or object after death? Most of us have keepsakes and treasures of our pasts tucked away to remember special memories. Ever wonder how much of our emotions and soul are connected to these objects?

The LaPorte County Historical Society Museum is not located in an old building. However, the construction of the building used materials from past area locations. Inside, visitors find a wonderful collection of antiques that were special enough to someone at one time to last for so many years. A historical museum such as this has the perfect setup for paranormal occurrences.

LaPorte County Historical Society Museum.

When Janet Lawrence was touring the museum with her Girl Scout troop a few years back, she became a believer in the paranormal. The girls were enjoying the tour and taking in all of the old relics with enthusiasm. Janet was enjoying herself as well. She'd always had a real passion for history and loved trips like this one. While the group was being given a guided tour, a woman of a very petite frame was following along behind the group.

This woman was wearing a long, dark skirt with a white button-up shirt. Her dark hair was pulled into a bun, and Janet thought that her clothing seemed quaint in an old-fashioned way. She always seemed to be behind the group or just around a corner but never directly within touching range of anyone. The tour was very well guided, and the kids asked several good questions. Being responsible for the girls, Janet was sure to keep a constant eye on the group.

At one point, the group was asked to go back out in the direction they'd come in. Janet, being in the back, was the first to turn around and head back out. As soon as she did, she came face to face with the petite woman. Before she could even politely move out of her way, the woman passed right through her! Janet had a feeling of heavy pressure pass through her chest, and she felt icy cold. She'd frozen where she was, standing for a moment, unable to move.

A soft push on her back from an impatient scout snapped her back to reality. Looking behind her, the petite woman was nowhere to be found. Feeling slightly embarrassed when she realized that she was shaking, Janet moved fast to the next part of the tour. For the rest of the trip, she couldn't focus on what was being said. Her eyes kept searching for the petite woman to reappear. She never did, which was a relief for Janet. She was certain that if she'd reappeared, Janet would have fainted. That would have been a great story for the kids to tell their parents later that night!

When they returned to their meeting place, they talked about the trip while waiting for the parents' arrival. Janet asked the kids to sit in a circle and go around telling their favorite thing about the museum. The girls called out many neat items, but Janet's attention was focused on one small eight-year-old girl. During her turn, the little girl said that she'd liked the shadow girl the best. When Janet asked what she was referring to, the little girl gave an explanation that caused Janet to take a seat.

She said that the shadow girl followed them on the tour and would turn from a person back to a shadow a lot. The little girl thought it was a very cool trick. Janet asked if any of the other girls had seen the shadow. None answered that she had, and they were disappointed that they'd missed it.

Janet decided that she would accept that at least she wasn't going crazy. Someone else had seen the woman who caused her such a scare. Even if her only witness was an eight-year-old girl who thought it was just a neat trick, Janet knew it had really happened.

Was the petite shadow girl haunting the building or simply revisiting an item she once cherished? We may never know, but if you ever have the chance to visit this fantastic museum, be sure and have your camera ready. Who knows if a petite young woman in a long skirt and button-down shirt will join you for a picture.

The LaPorte County Historical Society Museum building has been described as being in the style of Colonial Williamsburg, Virginia. It was built by Dr. Peter C. Kesling as a museum for his collection of antique and classic cars. Designed by architects Robert B. Drews and Associates, Inc., of Glenview, Illinois, it was first opened to the public as the Door Prairie Auto Museum on Thursday, September 1, 1994. The building contains historical references in its design, as well as historic fabric in its construction. The clock tower is an exact duplicate of the tower on the second LaPorte County Courthouse. That courthouse was designed by Chicago's first architect, John Mills van Osdel, and was constructed in 1847–48. This museum building incorporates double front doors from the Fildes Mansion, iron gates from Fox Woolen Mills and bay windows and storefronts from the 1898 Lonn Block, all of which once stood in La Porte.

LaPorte County purchased the building from Dr. Kesling in 2005 to transform it into the home of the LaPorte County Historical Society Museum. At that time, Dr. Kesling constructed a ten-thousand-square-foot addition to the back of the building to increase the room for displays. The result is a facility large enough to house the historical society's collections, with the Kesling Automobile Collection numbering over thirty vehicles still on view.

BRIAR LEAF GOLF COURSE

Bill Mann was enjoying a much-needed weekend of golf with his brother Randy at the Briar Leaf Golf course in La Porte, Indiana. The past few months had been difficult for Bill. He'd recently divorced his high school sweetheart. The divorce wasn't something he wanted, and he had fought it for almost a year. He was just thankful that his two boys were grown and in college. The reason his wife divorced him was because, she claimed, he thought he was never, ever wrong. She said that if he said it then it had to be true and that if he said something didn't happen then it didn't. This frustrated her until she could take no more. Sadly, looking back, Bill admits that she was absolutely right about him.

Bill received a much-needed dose of reality while he was teeing off at a difficult green at Briar Golf Course. He learned fast that he did not have all the answers. The day was a humid and cloudy July afternoon.

Bill and Randy looked like your typical golfers in their pleated khaki shorts and polo shirts, with neat pullover vests to finish off the look. Both men were in their late forties and of average height, with blond hair and brown eyes.

They had been discussing future business ambitions as they prepared to start an afternoon on the green. Randy tried to keep the conversation away from Bill's recent divorce. The previous day, Bill did nothing but talk of the divorce and put more balls in the water than Randy had ever known him to do, even when they were children. Bill was looking determined as he examined the scene in front of him. Taking a tissue from his pockets, he wiped his forehead and placed the tissue back in his pocket, or so he thought. He was about to tee off when he felt someone smack the back of his head! Turning to look back at Randy, he was puzzled. Randy wasn't near him, but who else could have done it? They were alone. He choose to ignore it and took a stance to tee off again. Suddenly, he felt a smack in the back of the head even harder than before.

Bill dropped his club on the ground and turned to Randy, letting out a loud, "Hey, knock it off!" Randy looked oddly at him. He claimed that he had no idea what he was referring to. Bill rubbed the back of his head, completely disturbed by what had happened. Was he so distraught over his divorce that he was losing his sanity? He had to admit to himself that Randy would not have been able to smack him and step back to where he was so fast. Also, Randy was not the sort who played these kind of games, in humor or otherwise.

Before Bill or Randy could even talk more about the matter, a very cold draft blew by them. Then a very odd thing happened. The tissue Bill had used was floating at face level in front of him. The tissue seemed to hover and not whip around in the breeze. He wasn't sure why, but Bill had a strong instinct to reach out and take the tissue, returning it to his pocket.

They made some lighthearted jokes about the matter, neither wanting to admit that the event unnerved them. Then they continued with their game. Bill now wonders if it was the spirit of a past groundskeeper angry with him for dropping his tissue on the ground. He is certain that he knows he was hit and has no answer for who did it. Boy, would his ex-wife love to hear this. He had no answer to what happened!

The strange occurrence at Briar Leaf Golf Course just gets more unusual. A few weeks later, when Randy was reviewing a video they had recorded of them playing golf, he found something that spooked him. There was a disembodied voice of a man saying, "Rodney, Rodney" in a stern way. Who was this man? Bill and Randy where the only ones nearby. This was really puzzling. Later, Randy found out that a previous owner of the golf course was named Rodney Mrozowski. Still, he found the whole event creepy and warns others to treat the beautiful golf course with the utmost respect because you are not alone on the green!

HESSTON STEAM MUSEUM

Ellen and Larry Hurst were vacationing in La Porte, Indiana, with their three-year-old son Ethan. It was Memorial Day weekend, and they were having a great time. Like most tourists, they looked through countless brochures at the hotel they were staying in, looking for fun things to do in the area. Traveling with a three-year-old narrowed downed their options a bit, but they didn't mind. Larry admits that having a toddler reminded him of the simpler things in life.

Early morning on Sunday, May 27, they were debating what they should do in the lobby of the hotel with brochures laid out before them. A employee of the hotel suggested that they might enjoy the Hesston Steam Museum. They decided that the museum looked like fun and headed off for a day full of fun and maybe a little adventure.

The day got off to a great start. The Hurst family arrived at the Hesston Museum at 11:00 a.m. and immediately enjoyed the sights of the old locomotives. At noon, they decided to go on a two-and-a-half-mile ride on a locomotive over wooden rails. This was perfect timing, as Ethan usually took a nap at this time of day. As the locomotive began its short journey, the scenery surrounding them was bright and vividly green. The smell of coal burning from locomotive gave them the illusion that they had journeyed back in time.

Ethan had fallen asleep on his mother's lap just as predicted. Larry put his arm around his wife. He had a pleasant feeling that all was right with the world. The ride was the best part of their vacation up to that point.

Looking out at the beautiful and almost enchanting land around them, Larry found himself wondering what the world may have been like a hundred years earlier. Blinking several times, he noticed a man walking toward them with a horse behind him. How fitting the image was as they passed by, he thought. A minute later, he saw the same man coming toward them, again leading a horse. How can this be? Larry was confused and looked back to see if he could still see the first man they had passed.

His wife gave his hand a squeeze and asked if he was okay. He asked her if she had seen the men they just passed, but she looked back at him, confused. Saying that she must have missed it, he went back to looking out at the scenery. Perhaps he daydreamed the whole thing. Taking in a deep breath of air, he blinked his eyes several times and cleared his vision. Larry sat directly upright in his seat. Coming toward them was the same man again. Quickly he turned to his wife and pointed in the direction of the man they were about to pass.

Desperately, Larry asked Ellen if she saw him. Again she replied no. She laughed, thinking that he was playing a trick on her, but stopped when she saw how upset he was becoming. Patting his knee, she told him to relax. Larry leaned forward and put his head in his hands. For the rest of the train ride, Larry kept his eyes closed.

When the train ride was over, he ignored his wife's pleas to forget what he had seen. She insisted that it was his imagination. Ignoring his wife, Larry approached a museum employee and asked if they had any people walking along the route of the train in old-fashioned get-up leading a horse. The employee shook his head no and chuckled. He told Larry that a few years earlier he had been asked the same exact question on Memorial Day weekend by a tourist. That tourist claimed to see a short man of either Native American or Mexican heritage. The man was dressed as a early 1800s settler and wore a cowboy hat low on his face. He led a beautiful black horse.

Ellen noticed that Larry had turned pale at the employee's description. Ethan was awake now, and she placed him on the ground. Putting a arm around Larry's waist, she realized that he was shaking. They thanked the man for his information and turned to find a place to sit down.

Larry needed to regain his composure. When they were seated, Larry told his wife that the description the tourist gave a few years earlier was exactly the man he'd seen that afternoon.

As it turns out, the Hesston Steam Museum certainly left its mark on Larry. When he returned home to Detroit, he decided to go back to school to further his education, majoring in American history. He hopes one day soon to teach the subject that has become his passion. Larry has a great respect for the past and those who shaped our great nation into what it is today. He is eternally grateful for the wake-up call the stranger gave him as he passed by on the locomotive thinking of days gone by.

The Hesston Steam Museum is located at 1201 E, 1000 North La Porte, Indiana. The museum opens for the season during Memorial Day weekend. Remember days gone by at the Hesston Steam Museum as real steam locomotives take you on a fantastic two-and-a-half-mile journey through deep woods, past lakes and farm fields and maybe even a ghost or two! There is a lot to do at the museum. Ride the ½-scale and ⅛-scale steam railroads. Both meander over bridges and through a charming wooded landscape and visit the old sawmill. Ghost hunt or just enjoy an affordable day of fun!

BELLA GUNNESS OLD FARM PROPERTY

If you live in the Midwest, then you have heard of the famous female serial killer Bella Gunness. There have been several magazine articles and stories printed over the years explaining the terrible murders she is said to have committed. In fact, a movie is in production recounting Bella Gunness's life. For those of you interested in the paranormal, it isn't going to be a surprise to learn that the murder site property is believed to be haunted.

The farm that Bella once operated in La Porte now has many homes on the grounds. While I was trying to determine where the actual farmhouse once sat, many residents in the area were not surprised to be asked. One senior in his nineties was able to pinpoint the actual location. He wasn't surprised to be asked about the Bella Gunness murders, nor did he find any humor when asked about ghost stories surrounding the area.

Knocking on his door on a Sunday afternoon, completely unexpected, was a joy to him. He loved the company and enjoyed sharing his Bella knowledge. He claims to have had an uncle who once worked on the

What was once the Bella Gunness farm property.

Bella Gunness farm for brief time. His uncle referred to Bella as being a determined woman with a motherly warmth. Still, there was always something odd about her that made him just a bit uncomfortable. Her temper was like a switch, and he witnessed her have more than one outburst. When the fire broke on the farm, he was no longer employed by Bella. When the bodies were discovered, he knew that Bella didn't fit the skeleton frame's description regarding her height.

The senior I spoke with lived very close to the original property. Over the years, he'd become used to hearing sudden screams in the night and seeing strange orbs in the yard behind his home. When asked if the property was haunted, his eyes twinkled. Smiling, he said that he didn't *think* it was—he knew it was. After shaking hands and thanking the friendly man for his time, I knocked on a door just down the road. A woman opened the door, not in a very good mood. After explaining to her that I was looking for information regarding Bella Gunness, she laughed—not a friendly laugh but something more sarcastic. She said that she was tired of people poking around the area and disturbing the peace. Then, right before shutting the door on my face, she said, "Damn kids trying to catch a glimpse of those strange balls of light. Things make my dogs bark at all hours. I am sick of it!" Despite her rude goodbye, she confirmed for us that she'd seen the lights that the friendly senior had mentioned.

A La Porte police officer claims to have been called to the property many times for the sounds of disturbances at a family home that was not occupied. Neighbors called police fearing that there were looters or trespassers on the empty home's property. One time it sounded like there were people fighting inside when the officer arrived on the scene. The inspection of the perimeter showed that there was no one around.

The murder victims were many, and perhaps still seek justice for their murders. If you are in the La Porte area and want to view the murder scene of the female serial killer Bella Gunness, think twice. One man claims to have been chased away by a shadow person around 3:00 a.m. one morning while inspecting an empty, nearby grassy area next to where the farmhouse once stood.

The history of Bella Gunness is one of tragedy. Known as one of the most prolific female serial killers in U.S. history, she is said to have killed more than forty people, including two husbands and all of her children at various points in her life. She also killed suitors and boyfriends and dissected their bodies like a butcher, feeding the remains to her pigs. She evaded apprehension by faking her own death by arson and was never found.

Accounts of Bella Gunness's life are often filled with misunderstandings and bad information. She was born on November 11, 1859, as the youngest of eight children in a small town in Norway (Europe, not Indiana). One story tells of an eighteen-year-old Gunness who attended a country dance while pregnant. That night, she was attacked by a man and kicked in the abdomen, causing her to lose the child. Her attacker came from a prominent local family and was never prosecuted. Accounts of the incident say that from then on, her personality changed markedly.

She came to America in 1881 and soon became "crazy for money" after living her life in poverty. In 1884, Bella married Mads ("Max") Albert Sorenson in Chicago, Illinois, where, a couple of years later, they opened a confectionery store. The business was not successful, and within a year the shop burned down under mysterious circumstances. According to

Bella's story, a kerosene lamp exploded and started the fire. No lamp was ever found in the ruins, but the insurance money was paid. It's likely that this money bankrolled the purchase of the Sorensons' home in the suburb of Austin, a house that was also destroyed by fire in 1898. Insurance was collected once again, and it funded the acquisition of another dwelling.

Mads died on July 30, 1900. That was the only day on which two life insurance policies for him overlapped. The first doctor to see Mads thought that he was suffering from strychnine poisoning. It is said that Bella killed her first husband in 1900 and collected $8,500 in insurance money. She was never charged. In the years that followed, four of her children died, many of which exhibited symptoms of poisoning. When her second husband died of a tragic accident in December 1902, suspicions began to swirl around Bella. Shortly thereafter, an adopted daughter, who was fourteen at the time of her father's accident, disappeared.

Over the years, several more suitors were lured to the family pig farm by answering "lonely heart" advertisements that she had placed in the local papers. Many of them were never heard from again. Finally, in 1908, the family home burned down under suspicious means. The bodies of Gunness's children were found inside, along with the body of a female who was believed to be Bella Gunness. The case was closed, but to this day, some are not convinced that the female body found in the ruins was that of Bella Gunness. The remains of the female found couldn't have been taller than five foot three, while Gunness was known to be five foot eight and weighed more than 180 pounds.

In 2008, Bella Gunness, Indiana serial killer, was exhumed from her grave due to suspicions that it wasn't really her inside of it. Over the years, many people doubted that she had cut off her own head and hidden it where it would never be found before jumping under a falling piano in the middle of a fire. Inside the coffin, they found the remains of three children.

Researchers have now also exhumed Gunness's three kids, who also died in the fire, and tests are being done to see if they were her biological children, which has always been a bit of a question. To shed some light on who might have been in that coffin along with Gunness, or whoever it was in there, some speculate that parts of the children were buried in one grave and parts were buried in another. If the children found in the Gunness grave aren't hers, who are they?

Bella Gunness children and victims are buried in this cemetery.

According to the researchers handling the DNA, there's about a 50-50 chance that the tests will work out. DNA samples have been sent to five different labs, but they feel that there may not be enough DNA left for conclusive results. If the tests are inconclusive, there is a backup plan. Permission has been obtained from Gunness's descendants to exhume Bella's sister, who is buried in California, so that more DNA can be extracted.

Also buried in California is another target for exhumation, the body of Elizabeth Carlson, who was awaiting trial for poisoning at the time of her death. Many believed at the time that she wasn't Elizabeth Carlson at all, but Bella Gunness herself! So far, the results have not been released. Considering today's technology, we hope to put the Bella Gunness mystery to rest in the very near future. Well, at least the mystery of how and when she died. We may never solve the mystery of whether she haunts the old farmhouse property.

PART III
HAMMOND

Wolf Lake Memorial Park

During the late summer of 2009, George Lancaster spent a lot of time fishing the waters of Wolf Lake Memorial Park. He looked forward to the peace he found when he fished. George claims to have been a nonbeliever in the paranormal and the legends of mystical creatures until one fateful day when that all changed.

George had been having a perfect morning. He'd left early to fish and was having a lot of luck. Then, suddenly, a natural instinct made him aware that something was not right. The fish stopped biting, and for reasons he could not explain, the hair on the back of his neck stood on end. George was terrified because he heard the water splash with some power behind the impact. He looked around for other boaters or someone along the shore—maybe there was a guy throwing something in the water. Turning in all directions, George realized that he was alone. The water splashed so high that he'd gotten wet! This spooked him, and he decided to move his small rowboat in another direction.

The distance he moved was interrupted by something that George will never be able to fully explain. He was terrified when he saw something come out from the water's surface! First it was a head, and then he directly saw the body. George can assure that the creature was very near his boat. He was about fifteen meters from the shore, and the creature was between him and safety. The creature was standing still, with its head up. At that time, George was sure that it was a sea monster, and one can only imagine how his hands shook. George said that his heart was pounding so fast that he could not breathe.

Thoughts raced through his mind. Was it was a dinosaur or a mystical sea monster? What did it eat, vegetation or meat? Most important to George in that moment was if it would become aggressive. George is a high school teacher and deals with problem sorting on a regular basis. This was one situation that he had no idea how to work out. Thoughts raced through George's mind when the creature began to move (or, better said, glide) just below the water's surface.

The creature swam in a wave, snakelike, and had sharp fins on its back. The skin seemed to be reptilelike, with dark green as the primary coloring. Most unusual were the neon colors of pink and blue that could also be seen along its slimy skin.

As the creature came even closer to George's boat, it made one of the most fearful sounds you can imagine. The sound was like a cross between a lion and perhaps Godzilla's roar, according to George. He watched it from the time when it came out to the moment it went completely under again and disappeared. The whole event lasted for about five minutes. George took this opportunity to move his boat toward the shore. When he was almost back on land, he heard the awful roar again. Looking in the direction where he caught his last glimpse of the creature, George saw it rise up again and skim the water. He watched the creature's many curves and bumps: three to four bumps, wavy like his body. Then that was it; the creature disappeared.

George left Wolf Lake and headed directly for home. The following day, he called in sick for the first time in more than ten years. The creature he witnessed had really terrified him. Today, he preaches that one should never say never. Who really knows what is out there. People search for a chance to witness what George experienced, but according to him they should leave it alone. There is not a doubt in his mind that creatures humans may presume to be only fictional are very much alive.

Purdue University–Calumet

Justine, like most college students, was always thinking about the future. She studied hard and, on the weekends, played even harder. She was well liked by her peers for her bubbly personality. Justine was always smiling and happy to meet new people. A lot of energy came from her small five-foot-three body and was contagious, as her friends would say. Auburn, shoulder-length hair and brown eyes that always seemed to twinkle best describes the pretty Brazilian student. Her first year attending Purdue University–Calumet in Hammond, Indiana, passed without any problems. She was really enjoying her college experience—that is, until she moved into the dorms.

When Justine learned that she had finally been chosen from the waiting list to receive a dorm room, she was thrilled. The first year, she had been sleeping on her cousin's couch in a very small one-bedroom apartment. Justine moved in fast and very quickly became friends with her dorm mates. Everyone agreed that she was great fun to be around. After about a month of living in the dorm, Justine began to complain of trouble sleeping. She told her roommate Sarah that she would wake up freezing several times a night. The temperature was set at a comfortable seventy-eight degrees, but still she was cold. This was the first odd thing that happened. Three months after moving in, Justine began to accuse Sarah of moving her things around. Sarah knew that she'd never touched Justine's belongings. This caused friction between the girls.

After several fights about Justine's things turning up after they had been missing, Sarah had enough. She found an apartment and moved out of the dorm. A new roommate, Stacey, moved in, and still Justine's things frequently disappeared only to show up later. This was becoming very frustrating, and Justine began to feel like she was the victim of a joke. She decided to just ignore the theft since the items always reappeared on their own. Still, she was not getting much sleep, and her grades began to suffer.

About six months after living in the dorm, an event occurred that inspired Justine to relocate. She was asleep when she heard her named called. Opening her eyes, she focused on her alarm clock. The time was 4:30 a.m. exactly. She felt cold but ignored the urge to stand and search for her blankets that must have fallen. A raspy whisper called out her name in the dark. The voice was that of a man, and Justine knew that it could not have been her roommate. Stacey was visiting her father in Ohio, and Justine was alone in the room. The feeling of fear filled her as she waited for the voice to repeat itself. When it came again, her eyes followed the sound to the foot of her bed. There stood a man in a long trench coat and top hat. He was shadowed, and she could not make out his features, but he was tall. She felt terror and thought that surely someone had broken in.

The man reached out a long arm and said, "Come with me Justine." That was enough, she screamed so loud that it woke up everyone in the nearby rooms. The man vanished back into the dark and was never seen again. Justine moved out the next day and transferred to Purdue in West Lafayette as soon as she was able. Reconnecting with her roommate Stacey three years later, Justine learned that the girl who took her spot in the dorm had the same occurrences.

Who is the spooky apparition that haunts the dorm? Justine is comfortable never knowing. She does suggest that if things turn up missing, relax; he will return it. Purdue University–Calumet offers dorms available for 376 students. However, if you are put on the waiting list, you might consider looking into some of the wonderful apartments for students in the nearby area.

THE HORSESHOE HAMMOND CASINO
(EMPRESS CASINO)

In 2006, Pam K. was working at the Empress Hammond Casino. She was working the gambling floor every weekend. On a particular Saturday night, Pam was startled in the ladies restroom by the image of a young woman looking back at her beside her reflection. Turning around, she realized that she was alone. When she looked back into the mirror, she was shocked to see the girl's image still staring back. Pam was startled but did not sense anything evil from the apparition. As she watched the image begin to dissolve, she smelled a lady's perfume begin to fill the restroom. Regaining her courage, Pam left the restroom. She immediately went to a respected co-worker and described the girl she had seen. The older co-worker had been employed at the Empress Casino since it opened in June 1996. She told Pam that she remembered a young girl fitting that description who had briefly worked in the casino. The young girl died in a car wreck.

Well, after a few weeks passed, Pam decided that she had just imagined the girl. That changed one Saturday night when a guest of the casino was left terribly shaken in the ladies restroom. While in a stall, the sink water had come on. The lady assumed when she heard the water that another woman had entered the restroom. The water stayed on for a long time. The lady soon caught the smell of cigar smoke. She got really aggravated by the odor. When she left the stall, the water was on but no one was there. She reached out, thinking the cigar smoker rude to not turn the water off. Before she reached the faucet, the water turned off!

This startled the woman, but not as much at what happened next. The woman noticed the face of a young woman appear in the mirror. She smiled a big smile and blew cigar smoke out of her lips. The smoke floated through the mirror and into the petrified lady's face. She screamed loudly, causing workers to run into the room. They found the woman pale and shaking. Pam was there to listen as the lady retold what had occurred. Why she frightened the guest of the casino and not Pam is a mystery. Over the time that Pam was an employee, she heard other tales of ghostly encounters describing a young woman. Some guests even claimed that a disembodied voice would whisper in their ear about what move to make when gambling. The happy winners cared not how crazy they sounded. Still there were some who complained of having their hair pulled when no one was around and their arms pinched. Needless to say, Pam was happy that the ghostly young woman liked her. This was an apparition that was selective. Pam never had another personal experience while working at the Empress Hammond Casino. She remembers her time there as the best in her life.

A note about the name: Jack Binion's Horseshoe Gaming Holding Corporation purchased the Empress Casino in 1999, and in 2004 Harrah's Entertainment acquired the Horseshoe, retaining the Horseshoe brand name. The casino is said to be a highly respected gambling location. The management maintains a sensational environment for its guests.

Regardless of whether you are looking for ghost or just a fantastic time, you will not be disappointed at the Horseshoe Hammond Casino, previously the Empress Hammond Casino. The original casino was closed, and a new casino was built. The old one was moved off to the side to allow the old ramping system to be disassembled and the new one assembled.

The floor space of the new casino is 175,000 square feet, and the gaming space is 108,000 square feet, containing more than one hundred table games, more than 3,200 slot machines, a keno lounge and a thirty-four-table World Series of Poker–themed poker room (the largest of its kind in the Midwest), plus elegant high-limit gaming rooms. The interior design coloring is consistent with a typical Horseshoe property, with black, gold, cream and a lot of crystal, including elegant chandeliers.

The Asian gaming area is particularly interesting; it was designed by Taki in New York City to appeal to Asian customers. It was made almost entirely from hand-carved wood from China, including the ceiling, and all of the furnishings have symbolic meaning and are arranged for maximum feng shui energy flow. It's called *le cheng* (happiness) and emphasizes the lucky no. 8, with an octagon-shaped baccarat room located off the main room, along with blackjack, pai-gow poker and pai-gow tiles, as well as two private, single-table salons for high-stakes baccarat. "It's all done to make our customers feel comfortable and lucky," says General Manager Rick Mazer.

An elevator and escalator lead to the second-floor buffet area and to the innovative 90,000-square-foot theatre called the Venue, designed by Montreal-based Scéno Plus. It transforms in less than two hours to accommodate anything from intimate performances to larger entertainment productions, as well as up to 150 tables for a large-scale poker tournament. The general admission floor holds 1,500 seats or 2,400 people, for a total room capacity of more than 3,300, plus a 3,500-square-foot VIP area with six box suites, each with three rows of seats and a full-service salon with couches and plasma screens.

Hammond is located on Lake Michigan in the northwest corner of Indiana, adjacent to suburban Chicago.

THE LITTLE RED SCHOOLHOUSE

About three years ago, Rob and Cadence were at the Little Red Schoolhouse on a Sunday afternoon. It was a warm August day, with high humidity. As they were standing outside the old building, they noticed a small child sitting at the entrance to the schoolhouse. The little boy was around seven or eight and had on a dark-brown tweed coat. He was leaning against the wall. He also appeared to have a bundle of books, with a belt wrapped around them, on his lap.

The small boy was resting his head back against the wall behind him, with his eyes closed. Rob and Cadence had not noticed the boy when they exited the old schoolhouse. They saw no one around who might have been the boy's parents. Cadence was expecting, and her motherly instincts were at an all-time high. She did not feel comfortable leaving the boy all alone outside. She walked toward the boy, calling out to him. He opened his eyes and raised his head. To Cadence's surprise, he waved to her and faded into mist.

Rob walked up to his wife to steady her shaking body. He too had seen the boy disappear, but his concern for his pregnant wife overpowered his fear. The couple returned to their minivan and headed for home.

A few weeks later, Rob couldn't stand it any longer and started asking friends if they'd ever heard anything odd about the Little Red Schoolhouse. After several inquiries, Rob was told about a co-worker of a cousin who claimed to see strange lights in the area. The man's name was Jason Gourp, and he had passed the area every night for more than a decade on his way home from work.

Rob called Jason and was surprised to learn of Jason's experience. Jason claimed to see what appeared to be small beads of blue lights, many of them going around in a circle. There was no other light source of any kind, natural or otherwise. Yet there were little blue lights outside the schoolhouse going around in a circle, many of them spinning. Jason couldn't believe his eyes. He pulled over and parked along the road's edge. In amazement, he watched for a few minutes, looking for an alternative light source that would have produced the blue lights, or some other explanation. There was none.

Finally, he called his wife, in a quiet voice, and asked her to drive over and look. Before she arrived, Jason watched the lights just appear to sink into the ground and gradually disappear. He couldn't believe it. Here these small blue lights had been going around in a circle for maybe seventeen minutes or so, and now that he was going to have a second person that could assure him that he wasn't crazy, the lights disappeared.

That was the first time he'd seen the lights, it was in 2000. Jason saw them several more times after that, and it was always at one o'clock in the morning. One night he had off and drove out there with his wife. This time she, too, witnessed the strange lights before they disappeared into the ground. As the years passed, the lights became a usual sight and no longer shocked Jason. He always looked for them, however.

This changed one night, when he got the scare of his life. Driving home a little later than usual, he approached the old schoolhouse. He did not see any lights but did notice a small boy with books slung over his shoulder, walking along the road's edge. Jason thought that it was odd to see a small boy of maybe seven or eight alone at two o'clock in the morning. He slowed down and pulled up beside the boy. Lowering the passenger window, he called out to the boy, "Kid, you okay?" The boy looked up with a angry scowl on his face. He did not respond but rather started to run.

Jason was surprised by the boy's behavior. He stopped the car and got out. When the boy heard the slam of Jason's car door, he stopped. He turned and ran toward Jason. Only about fifteen feet away from Jason, the boy threw his books hard at him. Jason ducked to miss the impact. The books never reached him, though. They had disappeared along with the boy! The sound of a child's mischievous laughter echoed into the night and sent chills up Jason's spine.

After that dreadful night, Jason never looked in the direction of the schoolhouse again. He is convinced that it is haunted. Rob hung up the phone and thought about Jason's story. The description of the boy matched the one they'd seen disappear. He decided not to share the story with his wife, who was so close to her due date. For him, it was enough to know that they had not imagined the whole ghostly encounter. After Cadence had the baby, Rob did tell her. She agreed that knowing that they were not alone in what they witnessed was enough. She had no intention of searching for the ghost. The mother in her was pleased that the old building has been preserved historically, offering a home to the spirit child.

The Little Red Schoolhouse was built in 1869, replacing a log schoolhouse. The schoolhouse is located in Hammond, Indiana, at 7205 Kennedy Avenue. The upkeep of this building has been historically well executed, and it is an asset to the Hammond community. The Little Red Schoolhouse is one of Hammond, Indiana's oldest buildings.

The John Dillinger Museum

One Friday afternoon, a study group from Chicago University was visiting the John Dillinger Museum located at the Hammond Welcome Center. The group members were studying 1930s gangsters. They were all concentrating really hard on their work when they heard a man's voice coming from the museum area. It was very clear. They don't know what he was saying, but they heard a man speaking very clearly. One of the students said, "Maybe a display is malfunctioning." Some of the displays had recordings that played if you touched a button. The group moved on and just brushed it off.

A few minutes later, they heard the voice again. All of the exhibits were off, and the whole place was empty in that area except for the student group. The group was nervous and uncomfortable about the whole thing. Of course, no one wanted to be the first to admit it.

After about half an hour, they heard the voice again, just vaguely, and the leader of the group was about to say something when the whole group started speaking at once, saying, "There's someone else in here, a man. I just heard him say, 'How many is out there?' He has to be in here."

When the group finished talking, they were shocked to see the silhouette of a man walk right past the group and into a wall. They were all educated people there, so it didn't make any sense how the man came out of nowhere and disappeared into a wall. Could the artifacts in the museum have residual energy connected to them? Perhaps the man they saw was the famous gangster John Dillinger asking if the Federal Bureau of Investigation (FBI) was outside? The museum has personal belongings of the famous outlaw. John Dillinger has been called a Robin Hood by some and was described as a caring brother and friend. Many have described Dillinger as not a violent coldhearted man but rather someone just trying to get by in a cruel and unjust world.

In 2009, Lydia Lopez visited the Dillinger museum with her four-year-old son. As she toured the interactive museum, she found herself greatly enjoying it. She was so lost in the displays that Lydia did not realize that her son had picked up a quarter from the ground and placed it in his mouth.

She was looking at the life-size wax displays when she felt a tap on her shoulder. A male voice sounded, "Ma'am, the lad placed something in his mouth." Lydia turned around and found no one there. Looking down at her son, she saw that he did indeed have an object in his mouth. She removed the quarter and gave her son a firm talking to. When the boy was calmed down, she remembered the voice. Looking around, Lydia saw no man in the area. A few minutes later, Lydia was holding her son and looking at a picture of Dillinger. Her son startled her when he spoke, "Momma he tried to take my money!" After some questioning of the boy, Lydia realized that the boy was accusing John Dillinger of taking the dangerous quarter out of his mouth! Could the ghost of John Dillinger have been visiting the museum himself and saved the boy from a dangerous situation? Not many people are inclined to believe in this sort of thing.

Regardless, if you are interested in ghost hunting or learning about the famous John Dillinger and other gangsters of the era, you will enjoy the museum. The John Dillinger Museum has been featured on CNN, ABC and NBC and has been the location of many paranormal group investigations.

John Herbert Dillinger, the unconquerable, the illimitable, had goofed. On the humid Sunday evening of July 22, 1934, he walked into a trap set by the FBI at a movie house in Chicago. He had been betrayed by a woman and was riddled by agents' bullets when he tried to run—cornered and killed just like any other unwise dope. Now, Lester Gillis (Baby Face Nelson) was Public Enemy Number One.

After Dillinger's death, things got no better for the existing array of motor bandits. John Hamilton had fallen in with bad company and was shot and dumped in an Illinois quarry. Van Meter, whom Lester was glad to see get his, went down under a hail of bullets in St. Paul. Around the country, others on Hoover's hit list perished: Bonnie and Clyde near Shreveport, Louisiana; Charles Arthur "Pretty Boy" Floyd outside Wellsville, Ohio; and more.

The gun-happy, top-of-the-list Baby Face Nelson, however, continued to sidestep an ongoing manhunt. But the ghost of Dillinger haunted him. The media kept comparing him to the late, great Indiana-born folk hero in uncomplimentary tones, aghast that the little gunslinger managed to outlive the much more adroit Dillinger. Even the FBI was calling Lester a punk compared to the elusive other, refusing to raise the reward on his head to equal that ever assigned to Dillinger's.

"I'll show them, I'll show 'em who's the better man!" Lester told Chase, another gangster. "Even if I have to rob a bank a day, they'll see who's the best!"

In August, the Californians took a trip to Nevada for a spell, lingering around the town of Minden, and then came back to Chicago. It was Lester's goal to staff up for what he hoped would be a bank-robbing spree. But he found no takers. The underworld had turned its back on him, for he was just too hot to deal with and, by reputation, too rabid to be practical. Ominous consensus claimed that he wouldn't live until Christmas now that he had stupidly come out of hiding.

FBI inspector Cowley soon learned that Lester and Chase had returned to familiar climes. Cowley was one of the bureau's "shining stars," proclaimed a report from the National Law Enforcement Officers Memorial Fund. "Only 35 years of age, [he] had managed to build quite a reputation for himself as a man with a brilliant, analytical mind and a tireless work ethic." With Melvin Purvis, he had determined not to let this murderer slip through their hands again.

From what agents were able to put together through eyewitnesses, Lester's Ford V-8 traveled frequently on northern Illinois highways between Chicago and Lake Geneva, Wisconsin, just across the state line. From time to time, they would hole up in one of the many resorts or hotels along the way. Unfortunately, according to author Richard Lindberg in *Return to the Scene of the Crime*, "FBI agents laid a trap at Hobart Hermanson's Lake Corso Hotel in Lake Geneva, but they failed to identify Nelson's car."

Cowley, enraged, ordered exclusive round-the-clock surveillance of all main and connecting roads in the vicinity—some seventy-five miles of farmland, small towns, picnic groves and pleasant lakes. For weeks, G-men traveled and doubled back over gravel roads, eyeing every car and passerby; they checked out filling stations along the way, diners and farmers' markets. Winter was coming, and the days were getting short, but the plainclothesmen were behind the wheel before sunrise when traffic was sparse and didn't quit driving until the sun set. In evenings, they loitered in the diners and at rest stops, hoping for Lester or Chase or the appearance of Helen, a known accomplice. They could recognize any of them by sight.

Along the rural stretch of Highway 14 on September 27, 1934, the FBI caught up to Baby Face Nelson and his friends heading south toward Chicago.

"With Nelson behind the wheel, the traveling party…were spotted by Agents William Ryan and Thomas McDade," explains Lindberg.

> *The FBI men pursued Nelson's sedan down Route 14, bur bullets tore through the radiator, disabling the government car…Moments later, a second federal car, a 1934 blue Hudson sedan driven by Herman Hollis and Samuel Cowley, approached them from the southwest.*
>
> *Turning their car around, the agents pursued…His fuel pump shattered by FBI bullets, Nelson crashed his car in the ditch and prepared to shoot it out with the G-men who took positions behind their Hudson automobile and a telegraph pole.*

Lester and Chase rolled from their stricken car, each toting a machine gun. Lester pulled his wife into the shallow gutter along the road and warned her to keep her head down. Chase, who crouched behind a clump of bushes, stared in amazement as his pal walked openly onto the dirt road, machine gun in front of him.

"Les, what are you doing?" he screamed.

"I've had enough of this cat-and-mouse! I'm going down there and kill them!" retorted Lester. Pumping the trigger without letting up, he moved forward toward the agents. Cowley and Hollis were no less surprised than Chase at Lester's show of lunacy. Crossfire erupted. The noise was blistering. The lunatic kept shuffling on, still squeezing his trigger in instinct even though federal missiles tore at his legs and chest and shoulders. His suit coat was shredded into rags. Half dead, Lester's aim didn't falter. Hollis fell back mortally wounded and wondering what from hell he had encountered; he continued to shoot until the nightmare downed him, too.

Both agents lay dying in a cornfield in the setting sun. Their killer, the monster, riddled with seventeen bullets in several vital organs, crawled to the agents' car. When he reached it, he hadn't the strength to lift himself into it. Chase and Helen raised him onto the back seat and rushed him to a priest. The good father could do nothing but offer religious consolation. If he knew for whom the bells tolled, he surely elicited the last rites from God emphasizing the maker's mercy to its fullest aspect.

Lester Gillis and Baby Face Nelson, one in the same, died that night at eight o'clock.

PART IV
PORTER

INDIANA DUNES NATIONAL LAKESHORE

UFOs at the Indiana Dunes State Park

The dunes have been known for decades to be a place of great beauty and mystery. Strange events of both ghostly encounters and UFO sightings are claimed to take place often. A visit to Indiana's prided dunes leaves no question in the mind of it's visitors why both human and otherwise would want to stay.

The sunshine was bright and the sky a deep shade of blue as Roger and Jess enjoyed their midday August hike at the Indiana Dunes State Park. The couple was on their honeymoon in Chesterton, Indiana. The weather was hot and sticky, but the two had cooled off in the waters of Lake Michigan before starting the hike. This trip had been planned for the last two years, ever since Jess had said yes to Roger's romantic proposal. They lived and worked in the modern concrete jungle of Chicago, Illinois. Both worked in the marketing field, at least fifty hours per week. This was the first marriage for each, and being in their mid-thirties, they were hoping that this soothing honeymoon in the natural beauty of the outdoors would result in the start of their family.

Roger had a very successful career as a result of his determination and drive. He was very serious and lived a structured life. Like Roger, Jess was also successful in her career. She planned every part of her life and

Porter, Indiana welcome sign.

believed in only what she could see. She wasn't one those women who believed in fairy tales. In Jess's mind, if you wanted something you had to work hard for it. This was a patient and rational couple. They may have been newlyweds, but they had been together for more than a decade. They were often mistaken for siblings, as they both had the same tall and lean frames with dark hair and eyes.

As they walked the sandy hills of the dunes, holding hands and laughing, the concrete world they came from seemed so far away. Laughing and talking about the future, everything seemed so perfect and in control. They were about to find out how wrong they were. Roger and Jess had just made it to the top of Mount Baldy. This sandy hill is 126 feet above the water level of Lake Michigan. The scenery from the top was magnificent. Roger was capturing a picture of Jess when he froze and his mouth fell open in utter shock. The smile fell from Jess's face, and she followed Roger's stare to the sky behind her. Illuminated in the clouds was a transparent object. When the clouds had parted just enough for the sun to shine on the object, the outline of what appeared to be a flying craft could be seen. This craft was completely silent as it seemed to simply float above Mount Baldy.

Roger claims that the object was shaped like a football and that no doors or windows seemed to be apparent. He thinks that the object appeared to be about twenty-five to thirty feet in diameter. Jess was the first to notice that all of the sounds of nature around them seemed to have been silenced. The object was an amazing spectacle that blended into the sky. Suddenly, a bright, blinding white light appeared, causing both Roger and Jess to shield their eyes. That was the last thing either remembered before waking at dusk off to the side of a sandy path at the top of Mount Baldy. The sound of children laughing first woke Roger. He opened his eyes and sat up. Passing by him was a family of four. The parents gave him a very disapproving look as they passed by the couple. Roger nudged Jess, whose head was on his lap, waking her. She sat up, feeling dizzy and disoriented. Looking at her cellphone, she noted that the time was nearing five o'clock. This was almost three hours after they had seen the UFO. Both were confused and had no idea how they found themselves waking up on the side of the path. No matter how hard they tried, the two couldn't account for the last few hours. To make matters more odd, Roger's Crocs were on the wrong feet when he stood up. He was certain that he wouldn't have put his shoes on wrong. He was thirty-six after all.

Roger and Jess were so disturbed by what had happened to them on top of Mount Baldy that they cut their honeymoon short. They were anxious to return to what they could explain, their normal lives. The couple does admit that after their experience at Mount Baldy in the Indiana Dunes State Park, they are certain without a doubt that mankind is not alone in the universe. "Think what you want and say what you will, I know what I saw!" Roger claimed on a final note.

Roger and Jess were not the only ones to have claims of seeing a UFO in 2009 at the Indiana Dunes. In late May 2009, a park employee who would like to remain anonymous claims to have seen two football-shaped discs land in the woods of the Indiana Dunes State Park about one to two minutes apart. They both landed in a similar fashion. Another worker was traveling west on U.S. 20 at about 6:30 p.m. The first one seemed to be "losing power," coasting at a downward angle toward the shore of Lake Michigan across U.S. 20, when suddenly it appeared to hit an "invisible wall," making the object stop in its path and appear to hover for a moment. He agreed with Roger that the UFO was football shaped and had a transparent appearance. The difference is that the park worker stated that the UFO seemed to flicker from appearing solid to invisible. Then it sank straight down into the trees. The employee of the park was still standing, amazed about what he'd seen, when a second one did the exact same thing! It happened a minute or so later, and the second disc seemed to land near the same area. The whole event seemed bizarre, and the employee wasn't sure at this point what he would even report. He headed in the direction that they appeared to go down but could find nothing. What could he even say about what he had seen without proof? He did not report it.

Later that evening, as well as the next day, there were F-14s and five black helicopters near the vicinity. The black helicopters were hanging

Indiana Dunes Lakeshore Beach.

around this area for a week after the incident. The park employee was curious about this, even several weeks later, and went on a search mission; he found the area in the park where he had seen them land. This time, his search showed him something that he had not noticed before. An extremely large tree had been twisted and "ripped" up by the root. The vegetation around the area seemed to be dying off, which he also found very odd. He had no explanation for what he'd seen, but it had an impact on his belief in the reality of UFOs.

A few weeks later, Tim Redding, a twenty-six-year-old male was walking in the national park on October 21, 2009. When he got to the top of Mount Baldy at 5:45 p.m., he looked down and noticed a shiny, metallic-like craft sitting on the ground about fifty feet away. The craft wasn't large and had a dome with a strange glowing light coming from within. The witness stated, "It sat there for about two minutes, then began spinning, and finally took off at an incredible speed, making a high-pitched whistling sound." He also noticed a strange smell. The object changed color to a bright red and, finally, a fiery red, heading higher and finally too far away to see. Then he looked at his watch, noticing that roughly two hours had passed. His memory and motor skills were affected by the incident, and he developed involuntary actions that included paralysis. Tim also had no idea how he had lost a few hours of his day or an explanation for what he'd seen.

Diana of the Dunes

When talking about paranormal activity regarding the Indiana Dunes, the most famous haunting is the story of Diana of the Dunes.

This story begins in Chicago, Illinois with a beautiful young lady by the name of the Alice Marble Gray. Alice was born to a very influential couple in Chicago. She was cultured, educated, and traveled to many places with her parents including one of her favorites around Chesterton, Indiana. The area, that she so loved, is now the location of Dunes State Park in Chesterton, Indiana.

There was not really much there when her and her family visited the area—just a lot of wooded terrain—but it was a wonderful place to relax and enjoy nature.

When Alice became an adult, she worked in Chicago as an editorial secretary for a popular magazine. Alice began having problems with her vision, which was deteriorating, and it made it impossible for her to do her job properly and she moved to the place that she had loved as a child, Chesterton, Indiana. No one knows the reason that she became such a recluse and lived alone in an old abandoned fisherman's cottage on Lake Michigan.

In 1915, stories spread before anyone was aware of Alice's existence on the lake, that fishermen had seen a beautiful nude lady swimming in the lake, this was none other than Alice. Alice loved this area and would often swim in the lake, take walks in the woods, and borrow books from the library. Before long, her nude swimming gave her the title of Diana of the Dunes, since her beauty was compared to that of the ancient Greek goddess Diana.

Alice met a drifter by the name of Paul Wilson in 1920. He had a somewhat shady past and was at the time of their meeting an unemployed boat builder. Alice was very happy or seemed to be in the beginning during the "courting stage" of their relationship. Wilson moved into the cottage with Alice shortly after the couple met.

This is where her story becomes sad. In 1922, the body of a man beaten and burned was found on the beach close by their home. Wilson

Indiana Dunes Beach.

was suspected of having something to do with the murder. The police questioned him, but did not have enough evidence to hold him and he was released.

After this, Alice and Wilson moved to Michigan City, Indiana. Here they made their living selling the handmade furniture they created and Alice gave birth to two daughters. He was an abusive husband and he would beat Alice terribly and treat her even worse. Alice died shortly after giving birth to her second daughter, the cause of death was uremia poisoning which was complicated by repeated blows to her back and stomach. Wilson disappeared and there is no mention of the daughters after this time.

Today, many have seen Alice again in her favorite place, the beach at Dunes State Park in Chesterton, Indiana. The ghostly figure has been seen running nude on the beach and taking a dip in the chilly waters of Lake Michigan.

PORTER WAVERLY BEACH

Leo Hubbard had been a Boy Scout leader for more than fifteen years when he took his troop to the shores of Waverly Beach in Porter, Indiana, during the summer of 2006. He had thought that he was equipped to handle all situations. This particular outing would prove otherwise. Leo and two scout parents had decided to take the troop of nine eleven-year-olds for a day of exploration and swimming.

The weather was perfect. The sun was shining, and there was a light cloud covering and a gentle breeze. The group arrived at the beach about nine o'clock in the morning. To their surprise, there was no one else along the beach. They began to explore the sand and natural erosion of the sand dunes that have taken place over time. Boys will be boys, and the occasional sand fight broke out, along with play fighting. Despite the behavioral interruptions, Leo felt that the kids were learning some information about the sandy beach that they did not know before.

As the group gathered in a circle for some information that Leo was about to share, they were stunned into silence. The scenery around them had suddenly changed. Instantly, there was hundreds of beachgoers

Porter Beach.

around them. The images of these people flickered like a loose bulb in a flashlight. The swimsuits they wore seemed to be from a different time. They were definitely overdressed for swimming by today's standards.

The scout group looked on in amazement as two men in old-fashioned suits and hats passed by on horseback. The group made not a sound, but the commotion of the ghostly images could be heard like a swarm of bees buzzing. Nothing could be clearly made out, but the joined noise was loud, filling their ears. Just as suddenly as the image appeared, it disappeared.

Blinking several times, Leo realized that they had all been knocked on their bottoms with the scene's disappearing. All members of the scout troop were shaking and breathing hard. None knew what to say, and Leo had no idea how to handle this situation. Nothing in the Boy Scout leader's manuals prepared him for porthole views into the past or ghostly encounters!

For those of you who are passionate about days gone by, following is some Indiana Dunes beach history.

Recreational development of the Indiana Dunes began in the late nineteenth century. By the early 1900s, development was concentrated in three areas: the Michigan City lakefront; Porter Beach and Waverly Beach, now Indiana Dunes State Park; and Miller, now in east Gary. Increases in disposable income and leisure time, combined with improved transportation, brought people to the Indiana Dunes to enjoy bathing in Lake Michigan and other lakefront diversions. Chicagoans in particular came to the Indiana Dunes. The Chicago-based Prairie Club incorporated in 1911 and in 1913 built a beach house for members. Prairie Club members and other beachgoers erected tents and rough wooden cottages for housing during their summers in the dunes. This early residential development had a minor impact compared to industrial sand mining that was destroying large areas of dune land. Alarmed by this destruction and by steel company land purchases, Prairie Club members and others began a campaign to create an Indiana Dunes State Park. Despite extensive publicity and advocates—including Stephen Mather, first director of the National Park Service—this effort was not immediately successful.

Resorts operating before the turn of the century included Tremont and the Mineral Springs spa and racetrack, the latter located near the present Worthington Steel plant. South of the lakeshore, G.W. Merrill's place at Flint Lake in Valparaiso was a popular fishing and swimming spot in the 1880s. In 1893, W.H. Leman reportedly built one of the dune land's first summer cottages near Lake Michigan and the present Mineral Springs Road. After 1900, Porter Beach drew crowds to dances and an ice cream concession. From Miller to Michigan City, from the west to the east ends of the dune land, fun seekers found diversions ranging from ferryboat excursions to boardwalk dances. Recreational businesses in turn spurred residential development that capitalized on the resort opportunities of the dune land as a sales tool.

The earliest recreational and residential development in the Indiana Dunes focused on three areas: the Michigan City lakefront; the section now encompassed by Porter Beach and Indiana Dunes State Park; and Miller in east Gary. Michigan City offered some of the first large-scale recreational developments along the Indiana Dunes lakeshore. A brisk excursion tour business had already materialized there during the 1880s. Tourists came to Michigan City by ferry or train to climb the Hoosier Slide, a two-hundred-foot-high sand dune rising at the current site of the Northern Indiana Public Service (NIPSCO) generating plant. By 1910, steamers carried as many as ten thousand passengers in a day to Michigan City's lakefront for Saturday excursions.

In 1889, the cry arose for public recreational development in Michigan City. Proponents of public lakefront access wrote to Michigan City mayor M.T. Krueger to support construction of a swing bridge at Franklin Street. The proposed bridge would open the Michigan City lakeshore to the public and enable "fine summer hotels and drives along the beach." Opponents of public recreation decried the proposal as an obstruction to recreation and a tax burden. Krueger, a strong advocate for public use of the lakefront, eventually procured the bridge at Franklin Street. More importantly, he authored and promoted state legislation authorizing cities and towns to levy taxes to establish public parks. The 1891 creation of Washington Park proved a major victory in Krueger's battle for public recreation.

The development of Washington Park and the Michigan City harbor heightened commercial interest in Michigan City's lakefront—a pattern later repeated around Indiana Dunes State Park and the national lakeshore. Just east of Washington Park, Sheridan Beach became one of the first residential developments in the Indiana Dunes around the turn of the century. According to Michigan City historian Gladys Bull Nicewarner, the Welnetz family built the first summer cottage on Sheridan Beach in the early 1900s. The Welnetz's wooden cottage provided a prototype for other Sheridan Beach summer residences, with a lakeside covered porch and a second-story dormer. A few years later, the Sheridan Beach Land Company platted Sheridan Beach Drive and other streets for a new residential subdivision. The land company's first speculative resort cottage, called Pioneer, was a stained shingle building, the first to be located on Sheridan Beach Drive.

Nicewarner points out that initial sales for Sheridan Beach property were slow "because people in Michigan City could not yet see the sense of building summer homes on what, to them, seemed like a wasteland of worthless sand." However a 1908 postcard depicts a cluster of cottages with broad gabled roofs standing on pilings at Sheridan Beach. The postcard was published by George Leusch, who sold souvenirs and ice cream from his store at the northwest corner of Franklin and Michigan Streets in Michigan City. Leusch promoted Michigan City with dozens of pictures of the lakefront reproduced on postcards, plates, match holders and other items. Promoters such as Leusch popularized the Indiana Dunes as a recreational destination and a possible summer cottage location for people in the Chicago metropolitan area.

To the west, the present Porter Beach area also experienced development near the turn of the century. In 1891, the current Porter Beach site became the Lake Shore Addition to the New Stock Yards as Chicagoan Orville J. Hogue recorded a plat in the Porter County Courthouse showing hundreds of twenty-five- by one-hundred-foot lots. Streets with Chicago names surrounded these lots: State, Dearborn, Clark and Michigan. Local researchers maintain that Chicago realtors tricked buyers into thinking that they were buying land near the Chicago stockyards, not inaccessible property platted over Porter County sand dunes. Many people abandoned the property they bought in the Lake Shore Addition, later selling their lots at tax sales.

However, others eyed the Porter Beach lakefront as a perfect entertainment spot. Although residential development proved slow, recreational attractions drew visitors to Porter Beach almost a century ago. "Porter Beach is now the center of gravity which is attracting the crowds from this part of Porter County," the *Chesterton Tribune* noted in 1904. "Every evening hundreds of people from as far south as Morgan Township gather at the beach, and have a good time bathing in the cool waters of Lake Michigan." However, the article bemoaned the lack of commercial facilities for beachgoers: "If some one would only put up sheds for horses, and a house for shelter for people at the beach, and serve something to eat, and provide some kind of amusement for the crowds, there would be money in it." Nine days later, an entrepreneur named Charley Swanson heeded the *Chesterton Tribune*'s call for commercial recreation on the beach. Swanson announced in the newspaper that he would serve ice cream on Saturday and Sunday nights at Porter Beach. He invited "all who desire to get cool and keep cool to come." About 1912, Elmer and William Johnson, two local fishermen, opened a rustic fish house at Johnson's Beach, east of Porter Beach near the present site of the Indiana Dunes State Park parking lot. The brothers later expanded their business, opening a restaurant serving popular fish and chicken dinners and offering bathing facilities.

SPRING HOUSE INN

The following paranormal event is retold by Jake Lowery. He had the misfortune of being cast in this eerie story and would love to forget the whole thing. Jake's bad luck now haunts his dreams.

The tale unfolds at the Spring House Inn located near Porter and Chesterton, Indiana. Jake was vacationing with his fiancée at the quaint and romantic inn during the summer of 2008.

It was shortly after midnight, just after a movie, when he and his fiancée took a stroll to enjoy the cool night air around the inn's grounds. The evening had an ambiance of romance, and they didn't feel like retiring for the night just yet.

After some walking, they stopped and sat a spell to enjoy the scenery. They were so intrigued with each other that they were surprised when a pretty little girl in white appeared before them. She had blond hair pulled

Spring House Inn.

back in a long braid and had on a long white dress with a large blue bow tied around the waist. She appeared to be crying.

Jake and his fiancée felt concerned for the child. They asked her what her name was and if she needed help. The child said that she was lost and that her name was Emily. The child couldn't have been more than nine and looked frightened. She told Jake and his fiancée that her mother was by the pool. They decided to walk the girl to the pool at the inn. They walked in silence. Jake could not put his finger on it, but something seemed odd about Emily. She walked just ahead of them and appeared to be very light on her feet.

Before the couple even made it to the pool, an orb of light appeared and turned into the transparent form of a woman. Jake was frozen in fear and looked on as the small child ran up to the apparition. Once she reached the ghostly lady, she turned and smiled. Then both of them disappeared into the night! Jake and his fiancée were frightened but felt strangely safe. The couple went back to their room and talked about what they'd seen. Both decided that despite the paranormal encounter they loved the inn and would finish their vacation. The rest of the stay went by with no more encounters. Of course, the couple didn't take anymore nightly strolls.

The Spring House Inn is located at 303 North Mineral Springs Road in Porter, Indiana. The staff is said to be wonderful and the accommodations immaculate. It is a fine vacation spot for the family or a romantic getaway for any couple.

WATER BIRD INN AND SPA

In the fall of 2009, a couple (who wish to remain anonymous) were visiting some friends staying at the exquisite Water Bird Inn. They were having a wonderful visit when suddenly the whole room turned black as night, despite that it was midafternoon. A cold draft blew through the room, and a scent of cigar smoke lingered in the air. A loud humming seemed to vibrate from the floor to the ceiling. The four adults remained still and were relieved when the room brightened again. They had no idea what had turned the daylight dark or where

Water Bird Inn and Spa.

the sound came from, nor did they ever find out. The Water Bird Inn and Spa holds a classy appeal and should be enjoyed if one ever has the time for an afternoon at the spa. The inn is located at 556 Indian Boundary Road in Chesterton, Indiana.

PART V

CHESTERTON

THE GHOST CHILD OF THE BAILLY HOMESTEAD

The children were running and laughing in circles as Rob and Alice looked on, smiling. The family loved their yearly summer vacation to the Indiana Dunes. This trip was fast becoming a family tradition. July was the perfect time of year to enjoy Lake Michigan's shore and explore the natural sites of the dunes. This family was the image of California, with their blond hair and perfect tans. Despite their love of their home in Long Beach, California, they loved Indiana's rustic beauty. Alice's dad relocated to Gary, Indiana, several years earlier, first introducing Rob and Alice to Indiana's rustic charm.

The day had been a perfect one. Surprisingly, Jake (four) and Blaze (three) had not gotten tired or cranky. The weather was a comfortable mid-eighties with a nice breeze. Rob and Alice were holding hands and sitting on the porch of the Bailly Homestead within the Indiana Dunes and talking about where they would dine for diner. The scenery was so beautiful around them that it felt like time had stopped. The Bailly Homestead's main house was a beautiful and charming example of nineteenth-century architecture. Suddenly, Alice stopped talking and stared at the children.

She watched the children playing and singing the classic song "Ring Around the Rosie" but noticed something odd. They were holding hands but not completing a circle. They each held out their other hand, as if

Chesterton, Indiana welcome sign.

The Bailly Homestead.

they held on tightly to a third child. As they spun around, they sang a version of the song that Alice had never heard before: "Ring-a-ring o' roses / A pocket full of posies / One for Jack and one for Jim / and one for little Moses / A-tischa! A-tischa! A-tischa!" As they sang the song for at least the fifth time, Rob yelled to them to come and sit for a minute. Alice blinked her eyes and tried to shake off the creepy feeling that suddenly was taking over her mood.

Jake and Blaze were giggling as they came over to their parents. Blaze was still singing the song and had a flushed face from his recent play. Alice knew that Rob was also experiencing a tingle of fear run up his spine. He sat for a moment more before taking Blaze's hand and saying that it was time to head back toward the car. Alice and Jake stood to follow when Blaze tugged away from his dad, "I have to say goodbye to my friend," he said with excitement in his voice. Before his dad even had a chance to respond, both Blaze and Jake ran toward the spot where they had just been playing their version of "Ring Around the Rosie." They seemed to be saying a goodbye to an invisible playmate, and Rob and Alice looked on in wonder.

Rob and Alice made eye contact and at the same time yelled for the boys to hustle up. They walked on in silence as the children hummed and pointed out different plants and bugs. When they had reached where they left the car, Alice got the kids some water bottles from the trunk. While they quenched their thirst, Rob asked the children about their invisible playmate. With bright eyes and eager smiles, both blue-eyed, towheaded children looked angelic as they spoke with innocence. Blaze said that his playmate was a little girl with hair the same color as theirs. Then he laughed saying that she was wearing a funny dress and hat. When Alice asked what he meant, Blaze said that the girl was dressed like the little statues Alice collects. Alice had been collecting Precious Moments figurines for years and knew that was what Blaze was referring to.

This seemed more than just the children's imaginations running away with them to both Rob and Alice. They decided to move along and not bring it up again with the children. About two weeks later, Alice was giving the boys a bath when they started singing the version of "Ring Around the Rosie" that they had been singing at the Bailly Homestead. Again, this gave Alice the chills, and she thought it odd that they would remember every word. She had never taught them that song, and when she asked Blaze to stop singing he replied, "Our friend said it will keep us safe." This made the hairs go up on the back of Alice's neck.

Later that night, as the children slept, Alice told Rob about the awkward thing their son had said. They both were puzzled about the words in the children's version of the song. They decided to Google different versions of the song. Both were shocked when they discovered that in 1883, Charlotte Sophia Burne wrote the version of the song the children had been singing. The song was published in *Shropshire Folk-Lore*. How the children would have learned this version of the song was unknown and only added to the eerie factor of the whole situation.

Who the ghost girl was may never be known. Perhaps she is a child laid to rest at the Bailly's family cemetery. Regardless, Alice and Rob's love for the Indiana Dunes will not be so easily given up. They will continue to vacation at the park, but Alice adds that they will no longer stop to rest at the Bailly Homestead. The song "Ring Around the Rosie" has the ability to make her knees to turn jello and hair stand on end. After all, many believe that the song originated from the time of the Black Death, which killed more than twenty-five million people in the fourteenth century. The words "Ring around the rosie" refer to the red rash that would first appear in a circle on the victim of the plague. The next line, "pocket full of posies," refers to the tradition of bringing flowers to put around the ill as protection. Of course, "ashes to ashes" refers to the death of the victim. Alice wonders what the words in the children's version stand for. Their imaginary playmate claimed that it was a song of protection. Could this be true? Alice and Rob hope to never find out.

The following historical information is from the Indiana Dunes Bailly website.

The Bailly Homestead, a national historic landmark, was the home of Honore Gratien Joseph Bailly de Messein (1774–1835). Bailly played a role in the development of the Calumet region of northern Indiana. He was an independent trader in the extensive fur-trading network that spread from Montreal to Louisiana and then ultimately to Europe. Joseph Bailly was one of the earliest settlers in northern Indiana. In 1822, Bailly set up his fur-trading post at the crossroads of several important

Inside the Bailly Homestead.

trails, including the Tolleston Beach Trail and the northern branch of the Sauk Trail. He provided a meeting place for Native Americans and Euro-Americans. Except for White Pigeon, Michigan, Bailly's trading post was the only stopping place for travelers and missionaries between Chicago and Detroit. Bailly acquired a formal title to the homestead and the surrounding tracts of land, totaling over two thousand acres, in the 1830s when the Calumet region was officially opened to Euro-American settlement. At his death, the title passed to his family. The homestead proper was left to his wife and segments of the acreage to each of his children.

In 1843, after the death of Bailly's daughter, Esther, management of the homestead was assumed by Francis Howe, the husband of daughter Rose Bailly. Under Howe's management, the homestead was again influential in the development of the area, as Howe sold timber from the land to be used in the construction of the nearby railroad. Upon Howe's death in 1850, Joel Wicker, husband to another Bailly daughter,

Hortense, assumed management of the homestead. It was under Wicker's management that the area surrounding the homestead was settled. In an effort to continue providing timber to the expanding railroad, Wicker recruited Swedish immigrants, then living in Chicago, to move to the area and operate the sawmill. Not only did the Swedes cut timber and operate the sawmill, they purchased land from the Bailly-Howe family and settled farms, bringing Swedish culture to northwest Indiana. Several log cabins, possibly dating to the 1860s and probably of Swedish origin, are located on nearby farms that were once part of the Bailly Homestead.

The homestead brings together an unusual combination of vernacular architecture with the imposing main house (featuring late nineteenth-century architectural detail), the rustic log and brick structures and the unusual family cemetery.

The Bailly Homestead complex is the last remaining site of its nature in the Calumet region, both in its capacity as a fur-trading post and in its vernacular architectural features and construction types. The Bailly Homestead was authorized as a national historic landmark in 1962.

THE CHELLBERG FARM

Over the years, many individuals touring the well-preserved Chellberg Farm have reported strange happenings. There have been reports of cold spots in the kitchen area and sounds of footsteps coming from empty rooms. Doors closing by themselves and strange knocking has also been reported.

Barb was touring the house in the fall of 2000 when she had a personal experience. She was waiting on the front porch for her husband when a chill went up her spine. The air around her suddenly dropped, which was odd because the weather had been in the lower eighties. She looked around and had a strange feeling that she was not alone. Suddenly, an unexpected voice sounded in her ear: "Wipe the mud off your shoes before you enter the house." Barb turned around fast, but no one was there. She was feeling very uncomfortable when her husband walked up to her a few minutes later. The house was open for tours that day, but Barb decided to continue on their walk instead. Her husband was disappointed but didn't argue.

The Chellberg Farm.

Years later, when asked if she had ever encountered anything paranormal, she replies that she had indeed and retells her tale of the tidy Chellberg farmhouse ghost. Many of those she shared her experience with had their own to tell. In fact, a few told of strange shadows and sounds at the Chellberg farmhouse themselves.

The Chellberg Farm represents a typical 1890–1910 Swedish and northwestern Indiana farmstead. The brick farmhouse was built in 1885 as a replacement for an earlier wood-framed house that was destroyed by fire in December 1884. The bricks for the new house came from a brickyard in nearby Porter. In the 1980s, the National Park Service restored the farmhouse to its turn-of-the-twentieth-century appearance, except for the dining room, which had been modified by the Chellbergs in the 1920s.

Anders and Johanna Chellberg, with their young son Charles, made the long journey from Sweden to this country in 1863. Traveling first by boat and then by train, the Chellbergs arrived here four months

Chellberg Farm outbuilding.

after their departure from Sweden. After their arrival in northwest Indiana, the Chellbergs became part of a growing Swedish community. They often gave other immigrants a place to stay and helped them find work. In 1869, the Chellbergs purchased forty acres of land and established their own farm. Forty additional acres had been added to the farm by 1874.

Anders and Johanna Chellberg had four children. After Anders's death in 1893, their son Charles managed the farm. Charles and his wife, Ottomina, had four children: Frank, who died when he was a year old; Ruth; Naomi; and Carl. When Charles died in 1937, his son Carl continued to farm until 1972, when he sold the property to the National Park Service.

THE GRAY GOOSE INN

The Gray Goose Inn in Chesterton is a warm and welcoming location for the weary traveler. Many have enjoyed their stay, and others have been startled by the ghostly image of a child. Matt Steward was staying at the inn one evening when he encountered the ghost. He had just taken a shower and was walking toward the bed to get the clothes he had laid out. That was when he noticed the most adorable child he'd ever seen. She was about three years old, with bright-red curly ringlets of hair. Her dress was an emerald green that matched her eyes perfectly. Shiny patent leather shoes and white-laced socks adorned her feet. She smiled at Matt as he stopped in his tracks and stared. A perfect dimple showed in her left cheek, and he noticed a twinkle in the child's eyes.

Before he could even respond, the girl vanished. He later asked a staff employee if anyone else had ever spoken of seeing the child. The

The Gray Goose Inn.

This page: Grounds of the Gray Goose Inn.

employee was very friendly and nonjudgmental. This put Matt at ease. He was told that there had been complaints of hearing a child's laughter and running on the property when there was no child present.

Despite the encounter, Matt stayed on. He was in serious need of rest and relaxation and found it at the Gray Goose Inn. All in all, his stay had been a perfect one, and the ghost child just added to the nostalgic feel of the place. The inn is located at 350 Indian Boundry Road in Chesterton, Indiana.

PART VI
EAST CHICAGO

AMERISTAR HOTEL AND CASINO

The sun was descending on a perfect day. The Monday afternoon was the sort depicted in children's storybooks. A picture of children playing beneath a perfect clear blue sky could easily be imagined. Birds chirping and butterflies gliding in the breeze put the finishing touches on the scene. This was indeed a very deceiving day, given the night that was to come for Tony Ramerez.

Tony was in his early forties but could easily be mistaken for thirty. He was six feet tall with a stocky build and a baby face. His olive skin and hazel eyes completed the description for saying that he was tall, dark and handsome.

Although most people learn by their mid-twenties that they aren't invincible and that life is short, Tony had yet to admit that to himself. He was single and had no children. He traveled for work most of the year. Tony did take time for golf, skydiving and surfing whenever time allowed.

Tony had no conscience and was disliked by many who knew him. Tony had played some golf that morning and enjoyed the casino at his hotel, the Ameristar Hotel and Casino, in the afternoon into the late evening hours. He was easy to spot at the gambling tables. Tony was always loud, cocky and annoying to those around him. After a night of drinking and throwing his money to the wind, he returned to his hotel room to get some shut-eye.

He had no sooner fallen asleep and begun to dream when he was awoken by a heavy breathing in his ear. Lifting his weary eyelids, he made eye contact with a ghostly white face. Anger shown in the eyes that met Tony's, and he was paralyzed with fear. The face had no body attached and no hair. He couldn't be sure if it was male or female, but he did know that he had never been more afraid.

The ghostly face stared as if it peered deep into Tony's soul. Then it smiled the most grotesque smile Tony had ever seen. Teeth gray and pointy appeared between thin dark lips. A cold sweat was felt on Tony's forehead, and his heart pounded against his chest. The head vanished in the blink of an eye, leaving behind an awful odor.

Tony regained control of his body and quickly dressed and left the hotel. Today, he leads a more careful life. He is always kind and considerate of others. He claims that his biggest fear is seeing that head again and feeling the evil that came from it. He believes that the entity could only have come from one place: hell.

EAST CHICAGO PUBLIC LIBRARY

You know the feeling you get when you feel that someone is right behind you? Or when you know that you are alone in a room and then you hear something or someone grabs your shoulder? That has happened to different patrons of the East Chicago Public Library. Juan R. has heard a whispering sound in his ear on more than one occasion. When he shared this with some of his classmates at lunch one day, it created a buzz of excitement. Several others spoke up about having different oddities happen at the library. One girl claimed to be looking through a magazine when she felt a tug on her hair by unseen hands. Another claimed to feel someone pull back on a book that she was taking off a shelf once, even though no one was there. All of these occurrences were small and easy enough for the teens to disregard. No one wanted to sound crazy and be made fun of by his peers. One girl claims that she was waiting for her parents to pick her up out front one evening after the library closed. She heard voices and felt someone moving around beside her. When she looked to see what was going on, there was no one there.

The teens agreed that they believed that their library had a resident ghost, but who could blame it for wanting to stick around? They did have one of the coolest libraries in the area, as far as they were concerned.

EAST CHICAGO MARINA

Janet Lewell felt like her ghostly encounter had to be shared. Hers was one of hope and left her feeling like life goes on after death. She was meeting a friend for lunch at the East Chicago Marina. As usual, her friend was late. Janet decided to take a walk around. The shoes she wore that day were not meant for taking a stroll, and a heel broke on one, throwing her off-balance. Janet thought for certain that she was about to land on her rear end when a hand reached out to steady her. Looking up, she smiled at her savior of the moment.

The man who rescued her from an embarrassing fall was very handsome, with caramel skin and a smile like that of Taye Diggs. He caused butterflies to swarm in Janet's stomach. She felt like a blushing schoolgirl as he smile back at her. "Those shoes are dangerous," the man said in good humor. Janet laughed at the comment and told him that she agreed as she took off her shoes.

The moment seemed perfect, and Janet found herself lost in his honey-colored eyes. What he said next snapped her out of the daze. "I usually don't allow myself to be seen, but you look so much like my daughter in a past life." He said it in such an easygoing way. Janet looked at him oddly, but before she could reply, the man winked and faded into the air. Janet was at a complete loss. Her mind could not get a hold on what had just happened.

Later at lunch, she shared the story with her friend. Of course, she was not taken seriously. Still, she knows what she saw and feels great comfort in the experience. The man was as real as anyone, yet he clearly disappeared like a spirit. Janet is convinced that life does go on. Furthermore, she insists to ladies that the East Chicago Marina has the best-looking man or ghost lingering in the area you will ever see. Don't forget, he is a gentleman, having assisted her.

PART VII
GARY

MICHAEL JACKSON'S CHILDHOOD HOME

Michael Jackson left a legacy that forever changed the course of music in modern society. From the roots of a family with exceptional talent that lifted them far beyond their humble beginnings to a historical musical career, Michael Jackson was indeed loved by many around the globe.

No surprise that many have traveled to Gary, Indiana, to see the famed pop star's childhood home, a home with very modest curb appeal that once housed the Jackson children, whose talent rocked a nation.

A ladies' reading group from Indianapolis decided to read a book regarding Michael Jackson after his sad death in 2009. One afternoon during a reading group meeting, the ladies discussed Jackson's childhood. There was a shared interest in his past, and the group decided to plan a trip the following Monday to tour Jackson's childhood neighborhood.

At about 10:00 a.m. the five middle-aged ladies pulled up outside Michael Jackson's childhood home in Gary, Indiana. The weather was cool, holding steadily at about forty degrees. The low clouds created a fog that seemed eerily appropriate as the group talked among themselves, mourning the deceased star. The small group emerged from the van and stood in front of the house. A few of the ladies felt uncomfortable standing on the property of someone's home, but the others were insistent to snap some photos.

As the ladies posed for pictures, a sudden cry sounded from nearby where the group stood. Everyone stood silent, searching with their eyes for where the cry had come from. Before words could even be exchanged, another sound, like children whimpering, came from just a few feet away from where the ladies stood.

Following the sound of children whimpering was the heart-stopping appearance of a golden white orb about three feet in diameter. The ladies grabbed hold of one another in fear. The apparition seemed to float like a bubble blown by a child, moving slowly back and forth in the front yard of the Jacksons' childhood home. When the orb was only a few feet from the ladies, it dissolved like a bubble being popped. Hundreds of gold speckles evaporated into the air like a mist.

One of the ladies screamed, breaking the frozen stance they had held. The ladies, as fast as possible, piled into the van and drove away. Some paranormal experts believe that a tragedy or abusive home can stamp that negative energy forever onto the location where the events occurred.

That the Jackson children suffered an abusive childhood had been well publicized. Could the pain they suffered as children be replaying forever throughout time? Did the abuse they suffered as children stamp itself on the Jacksons' childhood home, creating a residual haunting? One is only left wondering.

Globally, it has been prayed that Michael Jackson has found peace. Reports after his death have been made claiming that his apparition has been seen at Michael Jackson's beloved home, Neverland. This author can only hope that his spirit simply chooses to revisit a home he was known to love—a source of pride that was his personal heaven—and that peace has at last found the obsessed perfectionist. Michael Jackson, rest in peace.

TRUMP HOTEL AND CASINO

In December 2009, Rene and Nita Santos ware having a great time at the Trump Hotel and Casino. The couple considered this particular casino the best in Indiana. Nita believes that it has a magic all its own. She claims to be sensitive and that there is a warm-hearted spirit of a young woman who haunts the gambling floor. If a gambler has good intentions, the ghost will allow him the instinct to win. However, if the ghost feels that the gambler will use the winnings for ill will, she will jinx them. According to the couple, all one has to do is enter the casino to notice that the element of individuals gambling and having a good time are of good nature. Nita claims that the spirit of the ghostly woman keeps the riffraff away. Regardless of whether one believes in Nita's theory, one has to admit that the casino is of excellent quality.

MAJESTIC STAR HOTEL AND CASINO

The following paranormal encounter is told by Jeff Morris. He is a fifty-nine-year-old family man and a pastor. Although he now believes in the paranormal, he holds a firm belief and faith for God's wisdom. Jeff told his story with caution, stopping many times to assure that he is being 100 percent honest, and he still can barely believe how it sounds himself.

In the suite we were staying in was my brother and his wife, as well as myself and my children, ages twenty-one and twenty-two. I awoke around 3:30 in the morning to the sensation of a pressure on my side, kind of pushing me down. I thought it might be my son, who was bunking with me, pushing me down. I raised my arm out to try to push off whatever was on top of me. I felt something substantial but definitely not my son. It was at that time I began to get frightened.

I was laying on my side, so I turned my head to my right shoulder to get a glimpse of what was on top of me. I saw a large dark funnel of no substantial shape. I heard a mocking laugh. I struggled, to no avail. I decided to let the entity know that they should get off of me in the name of Jesus Christ. The funnel suddenly hit the ceiling and disappeared.

There I was, very frightened, hoping it was a dream. I decided to sleep sitting up on the bed. I woke nobody up, as I felt like my sister-in-law would think I was nuts, and I didn't want to scare my kids. So I tried going back to sleep. This is when I felt hands all over the front of me, pushing and pulling. I knew I was sleeping when the second attack began as the sensations began to wake me up.

I cried out, and this woke my sister-in-law. She said she looked over at me in bed and saw that I had a dark figure over me, with its "arms" wrapped around me. My brother then heard my cry, turned on the light and asked me if I was okay. I told him that I was definitely not okay. My sister-in-law told my brother what she saw and that it seemed to shoot up into the ceiling when the lights went on. I told him what I experienced.

Unfortunately, we were looking at another night in the same room already paid for. Thus, I didn't sleep and basically played "night watchmen." I was ready with my camera should the entity return. The only thing that happened was my daughter crying in her sleep, and I could see nothing bothering her from my viewpoint. Later, she revealed that she had a nightmare about a dark man that was making it hard for her to breathe.

I would like to clarify [that] I was on no medications, had not drunk any alcohol during this trip. This was the scariest thing to ever happen to me, and because of what my sister-in-law witnessed as I cried out leads me to believe it may be paranormal. My concern is: will other people suffer this same malady in that room? I definitely believe it was malevolent. Another question I am left with is: is this the attack from a "shadow person"? My best friend told me I should have asked for a different room. I was too worried the staff would think I was crazy! The hotel was beautiful and very well managed. This was definitely not the kind of place that one appeared at the front desk with nutty stories. The Majestic Start Casino and Hotel is sensational and, needless to say, despite the evil entity, we had a wonderful time. I will return without fear. After all, I have God on my side.

What Jeff Morris and his family may have encountered could very well have been a shadow person. At first they appear only out of the corner of your eye, furtively darting out of view when you turn to look straight at them. Did you really see them? Shaking the image out of your head, you assume that it was some peculiar anomaly of your eyesight; however, the feeling still lingers that someone continues to watch you. For weeks, months or years, the fast, dark movements in your peripheral vision are dismissed until it finally happens without warning. Sometimes it appears as the mere silhouette of a person, usually male, but generally lacking any other characteristics of gender. However, in no way does the description end there. There are "hated" shadow beings, hooded shadows, cloaked ones and solid or wispy, smoky types. Some are seen only from the waist up. Others clearly have legs that are seen fleeing from their observers. They dart into corners, through walls, into closets or behind television sets, bushes and buildings. Sometimes they simply fade into the dark recesses of the night.

PART VIII

NOTRE DAME AND CROWN POINT

UNIVERSITY OF NOTRE DAME

Jim was a first-year student at Notre Dame. His parents had always talked to him about attending the prestigious university. Both his father and grandfather had graduated from the school, and Jim always knew that he would keep the family tradition going. Like most young men, he was excited about being on his own for the first time.

When he first entered the dorm at which he would be staying for the next year, he was filled with a sense of adventure. His dorm room was small but cozy, with just enough space. The first few days were very busy while he unpacked and adjusted to his new schedule. On his third day, Jim was organizing his belongings when a cold draft suddenly blew past him. He shivered and put on a sweatshirt. This wasn't very odd considering that fall was fast approaching. However, after he put on his sweatshirt, it suddenly became very warm. He was certain that the temperature had shifted at least ten degrees in a matter of a few minutes. He couldn't put his finger on why, but he does remember that this moment was the first time he got the creeps in his dorm room.

Initially, Jim had thought that he'd really lucked out not having a roommate, but as time went on he found himself wishing that he had one. On a December night, Jim was woken at about 3:00 a.m. to the soft sound of a female humming. He sat up in bed and immediately turned on the lamp beside his bed. When the light filled the room, the humming stopped. Looking around, he saw nothing out of the ordinary. Thinking that maybe the sound had come from another dorm room, he turned off the light and lied back down. Within a few minutes of the light going off, the humming returned. The sound was soft and didn't seem to have any particular pattern. This time when Jim sat up in bed, he didn't turn on the light but instead listened. The humming seemed to be coming from right beside his bed. After a few more minutes, he turned on the light, and the sound stopped right away again. This continued until the first rays of morning light filtered in through the window.

After the first night of the humming, it became a regular occurrence. Jim learned to ignore it since it didn't seem to cause him any harm. He was embarrassed to tell any of his friends about the strange humming and kept it to himself. As the school year progressed, Jim was really struggling with his studies as a result of not getting enough sleep. He started drinking and doing drugs in an attempt to deal with his anxiety. The change in Jim was noticed by his parents, and they were finally able to get Jim to open up and tell them what was bothering him. The humming wasn't the only thing he couldn't explain. Jim also felt an awful sense of doom overcome him. A few times while studying at his desk, someone would tap him on the shoulder. When he would turn around, no one was there. He was alone. At other times, the alarm clock or TV would turn on by themselves. The stress was really becoming too much for Jim. Some days, he would feel sick to his stomach and very dizzy, but when he would leave the room he would feel fine right away.

Jim told his parents about the strange events happening in his dorm room. They suggested to Jim that he relocate. Taking his parents' advice, Jim changed dorms. Right away Jim felt better. He felt like a cloud had been lifted from him. His mood was much more positive, and he slept wonderfully. The change brought on better grades, and he eventually graduated with honors.

Although Jim never found out who or what haunted his first dorm room, he is a firm believer in the paranormal. He is certain that paranormal entities can have a drastic effect on a person's life.

CROWN POINT JAIL

In 1882, the Sheriff's House was built to serve a succession of elected sheriffs for seventy-six years until 1958. It is a two-story brick building designed in Second Empire Victorian style, complete with deeply sloping mansard roofs. Thanks to the efforts of the Sherriff's House Foundation of Indiana, the building is currently being refurbished and renovated. The Northwest Indiana Building and Construction Trades Council has been generous in this effort by donating workers and materials for needed plastering, carpentry, electrical work, roofing and other areas needing a facelift.

In 1926, a large two-story brick jail building was added on to the Sheriff's House, making it more convenient to keep an eye on people in custody—bringing work home from the office, so to speak. Thus, the back part of the Sheriff's House was called the Lake County Jail.

The large two-story brick jail, with its own tall chimney, is located in the back of the building. It isn't in very good shape inside, but it is also having work done so it can be used for storage; it still won't be a part of the tour for the public, though.

Lake County Jail became known as the place from which John Dillinger made his fantastic escape in 1934. After John Dillinger was caught by authorities in Tucson, Arizona, on January 30, 1934, Lake County was first in line to drag him into court for a trial, because he was involved in a bank robbery at which innocent people were killed.

Bank robber and gangster John Dillinger knew that he was headed for death if he remained in the hands of the state. While in custody in this jail, he used the materials at hand to help him temporarily foil the wheels of justice. Using jail-issued razor blades, John carved a gun from a wooden washboard, staining it with black shoe polish. He then threatened his guards with the fake gun, helped himself to a real automatic, and took hostages temporarily to ensure his escape to Illinois. All of this was for nothing, as it didn't get him very far. The following Sunday after his bold escape, John Dillinger was killed by federal officers outside of the Biograph Theater in Chicago.

Though this jail was closed since the 1970s, an entity or two is stuck. Perhaps a prisoner is still being held here though in reality it was freed long ago from being in custody in this jail. Personal reports from the living and photos taken of a jail window and inside the building point to this being's apparent existence.

Or perhaps the entity is a guard or a law officer who was fooled by Dillinger's fake gun. The back portion of the Crown Point Sherriff's House building and Lake County Jail has had cell doors that have the habit of opening and closing by themselves. Also, some unseen entity seems to be trying the bars of cells, looking for a loose one, because the living have heard the bars rattling in cells with no living person in sight. As is the case in other haunted places, the unseen entity is fascinated with electricity and likes to turn the lights on and off. Voices and footsteps have been heard in the old jail when no one living was anywhere near the jail area.

During some reconstruction of the building, a man was walking his dog past the front door. Suddenly, he heard a commotion from inside, and although the doors did not open, a noise sounded like they did. A rush of cold air came at the man, and he was knocked down like someone had pushed him. A voice said, "Pardon me," and the man's dog barked violently! No one was around, and the man stood up back on his feet. All had gone quiet again, and the temperature had warmed back up. Could that have been the residual energy of Dillinger's famous escape from the Crown Point Jail replaying for all eternity?

PART IX
SOUTH BEND

SOUTH BEND REGIONAL AIRPORT

The South Bend Regional Airport is an asset to the surrounding community. There is a lot of history at the airport, and so it comes as no surprise that reports of apparitions and ghostly objects have been experienced. Witnesses have reported seeing the ghostly image of a German-made zeppelin of the 1920s fly over the airport on hazy days. Other reports note that old aircrafts of the 1930s approach the runway to land before disappearing. On other occasions, the apparition of a man in a World War II flight jacket and goggles has been seen pacing at different locations in the airport. One woman claims to have pet a cat before entering the airport, only to have it disappear before her very eyes. Despite these abnormities, it is not hard to imagine why the dead would haunt an airport. If there is any truth in the theory that apparitions gain strength from living emotions, an airport would be the place to find a charge. People arriving and leaving often have friends and relatives at the airport and strong emotions are often present. Following is some historical information from the airport's website.

A tradition peopled by great men and women of vision. That's South Bend Regional Airport. Ever since the dashing French aviator, René Simon, first touched down in South Bend in 1911 marking the area's first recorded airplane flight, the Michigan region has played an exciting and often pivotal role in aviation history. For more than sixty years, beginning in 1929 when local industrialist Vincent Bendix began constructing the airport, South Bend Regional Airport has been a proud participant in that rich tradition and heritage. Back then, the airport logged a handful of flights on a chalkboard that was posted out of doors, near a dirt runway.

In 1936, Amelia Earhart lands her Lockheed Electra at Bendix Field just a few months before her aircraft disappeared in an attempted around-the-world flight. The city purchases Bendix Field from Vincent Bendix for $198,000. The field is renamed Bendix Field–St. Joseph County Airport; after ownership is transferred to the county.

In 1960, President Eisenhower arrives at the airport. Presidents Johnson, Nixon, Ford, Carter, Reagan, Bush and Clinton have all landed at Michigan Regional.

Skipping ahead to 2007, a milestone is reached on SBRA's long-range Master Airport Improvement Plan, with the completion of an 1,100-foot addition to the North-South runway for a total of 7,100 feet.

The Air Traffic Quarterly Report lists SBRA as the top airport in the Great Lakes Region in domestic load factor (percentage of seats filled on each flight), exceeding both O'Hare and Midway airports in Chicago.

STANLEY COVELESKI REGIONAL STADIUM

Chris and Steven had both worked maintenance at the stadium when it first opened. The men were thrilled to be working there and took their jobs seriously. The stadium at the time was new, and when strange things started to happen, the men did not know what to think. On one occasion, the men had been cleaning the restroom when all of the water faucets turned on at once. They went off at exactly the same time. Other workers complained of lights flickering and things disappearing. Still, they decided that complaining about the chilling events was not worth losing their jobs.

As the years passed, the strange events continued. The pop dispenser would suddenly malfunction, and the park lights would flicker. Fights sometimes started when hair was yanked and no one spoke up to doing it. That was stuff that both Chris and Steve could deal with. When the shadow people began making themselves known, though, that was too much for the men.

One day, Chris and Steve were again cleaning the men's restroom when the lights began to flicker. Both men looked around and were horrified to see a shadowed image in the mirror. They were alone in the bathroom. They gave their notice and found other jobs not long after. Over the years, rumors that the stadium is haunted have served as gossip. Let's just hope that the ghosts are rooting for the home team.

Stanley Coveleski Regional Stadium was built in 1987 for $11 million under the leadership of then mayor Roger O. Parent. The facility is owned by the City of South Bend and managed by the South Bend Parks & Recreation Department. Stanley Coveleski was a hall of fame pitcher who settled in South Bend after his successful baseball career came to an end in 1929. The stadium is now affectionately known as "The Cove." The five-thousand-seat stadium is worth an estimated $35 million to $40 million today.

The stadium is home to the South Bend Silver Hawks, a Class A minor league baseball team affiliated with the Arizona Diamondbacks. The Silver Hawks, who play in the Midwest League, were named in homage to the Studebaker Silver Hawk, once made in South Bend. Originally affiliated with the Chicago White Sox, the team switched to the Diamondbacks in 1997.

Called "the grandfather of the modern ballpark" by www. ballparkreviews.com, Coveleski Stadium provided a design template for a move in recent years to bring ballparks back into city downtowns. HOK Sport Inc. (now Populous), architect of Coveleski Stadium, also designed Oriole Park at Camden Yards in Baltimore and Cleveland's Jacobs Field.

ABOUT THE AUTHOR

D orothy Salvo Davis was born in Massachusetts. She spent her earliest years in New England and moved to south Florida when she was still a child. Raised in an Italian American family, Davis is very open-minded, and Fort Lauderdale's many cultures are reflected in her writing.

Her first book, *Ghost Stories of White County*, set her on a path to document the paranormal. She is also the author of *Haunted Lafayette* and *Broward County Florida Haunts*. Having a true love for history, Davis feels that it is important to remember those who created the world as it is today. When researching the history of a paranormal site, she does so with respect for the location's past. Currently she resides variously in Indiana and south Florida with her husband and children. Watch for many great titles coming from this ambitious author...

Visit us at
www.historypress.net